THE COMMONWEALTH AND INT

Joint Chairmen of the   SIR ROBERT ROBINSON, O.M., F.R.S.
Honorary Editorial Advisory   London
Board   DEAN ATHELSTAN SPILHAUS
Minnesota

Publisher   ROBERT MAXWELL, M.C., M.P.

ON TEACHING FOREIGN LANGUAGES TO ADULTS

ON TEACHING FOREIGN LANGUAGES TO ADULTS

A Symposium

edited by

MARGARET LOWE, Ph.D.

and

JOHN LOWE, Ph.D.

Director of Extramural Studies,
University of Edinburgh

PERGAMON PRESS

OXFORD · LONDON · EDINBURGH · NEW YORK
PARIS · FRANKFURT

Pergamon Press Ltd., Headington Hill Hall, Oxford
4 & 5 Fitzroy Square, London W. 1
Pergamon Press (Scotland) Ltd., 2 & 3 Teviot Place, Edinburgh 1
Pergamon Press Inc., 122 East 55th St., New York 22, N.Y.
Pergamon Press GmbH, Kaiserstrasse 75, Frankfurt-am-Main
Federal Publications Ltd., Times House, River Valley Rd., Singapore
Samcax Book Services Ltd., Queensway, P.O. Box 2720 Nairobi, Kenya

Set in 11 on 12 pt. Plantin
Printed in Great Britain by
The Anchor Press Ltd · Tiptree, Essex

Contents

Introduction

IN a new version of a well-worn scene a recent London theatrical success showed German soldiers singing carols to their British adversaries in the Flanders trenches and calling out to them in English.

'They're good linguists!' a British soldier approves.

'Yes,' his companion replies. 'They learn it at school.'

Half a century later, when a knowledge of foreign languages is no longer an esoteric qualification but a commercial necessity, a European gathering at almost any level is likely to provoke both reactions. The Englishman, even when well educated, tends to stand out as an inferior linguist. The simplest investigation reveals that unless he went into the Arts side of a sixth form he usually gave up studying any foreign language at the age of sixteen: that is, after GCE 'O' level; the Scandinavian or German, who dazzles with his fluency, is found to have continued with two or more languages as a compulsory part of his school-leaving certificate, taken at the age of nineteen, or even later.[1]

From this fact alone it would follow that problems connected with the teaching of foreign languages to adults are particularly relevant in the United Kingdom. Our normal system of training for most professions does not automatically include a thorough grounding in even one foreign language. Unless he is preparing to specialize, anyone wishing to be a proficient linguist is likely,

[1] Relevant figures are: *Denmark* (average age 19) French and one other modern language compulsory for all except language specialists, who take three; *W. Germany* (18 or 19) at least two modern languages compulsory for all except scientists, who must pass in at least one; *Holland* (19) French, German and English compulsory for all; *Sweden* (20) English compulsory for all, *plus* optional German or French for scientists and Russian with French or Spanish for those preparing for commerce; four modern languages are possible on the language side. In *Denmark* and *Sweden* compulsory Latin may be replaced by Russian.

as things stand, to address himself to the task when his professional qualifications are already acquired; that is to say, as an
adult, and through agencies outside the schools and universities.
This being true of the professions, how much more must it
apply to the rest of the community.

Changes in our whole system of 'O' and 'A' levels seem
inevitable, but even if they were introduced in the near future
the shortage of good linguists from which the country is at
present suffering would necessarily continue for some time. In
any case, when more instruction in the schools eventually
relieves the pressure for emergency training in the more commonly known European languages, adults will still be demanding
to learn foreign tongues. Mandarin Chinese, Russian, Japanese
—the possibilities are endless, bringing in their train problems
which are likely to occupy us indefinitely.

But to return to the situation as it exists in this country
today, it is well known that the demand from adults for language instruction has increased beyond all expectations since
the war. It is also often suggested that the national provision
is not only out of date in its methods but inadequate in its
scope. To what extent are these charges justified? How, in fact, are
we dealing with the task of teaching foreign languages to adults?

The editors have thought it valuable to attempt an answer to
questions such as these by assembling information concerning
the nature and extent of the problem of language teaching to
adults in England and Wales in the hope of providing a guide to
the present demand and to the machinery available to cope with it.
In addition, we were particularly interested to obtain from experts
in the field descriptions and discussions of methods which they
use, together with indications of the main lines which thought
and experiment are following at the present time and recommendations for the future.

2. Techniques and Experiments

The task was undertaken in the knowledge that although
British reactions to the problems of language teaching have

indeed been slow (perhaps understandably so), much thought and attention have been given to the subject by individuals. Many language tutors are also at present reappraising their own efforts, recognizing that their results, with adults as with children, are often lamentable, accepting the rising vocational demand as a test of their mettle and whole training, seeking for an opportunity to use the new techniques that have been so much praised. The wide publicity given to aural and audio-visual aids has, to some extent, been a disadvantage, for it is particularly in the field of language learning for adults that there has been most uninformed talk of miraculous overnight results, leading inevitably to disenchantment. It seems scarcely necessary to say that the experienced practitioner has never conceived the new equipment to be anything more than a highly valuable aid; nor would he willingly throw overboard all the so-called 'traditional' methods of language teaching.[1] The fact remains that radical improvements in our techniques and in our results are certainly called for. A thorough-going rejection of the Anglo-Saxon myth of the 'poor linguist', re-thinking on the part of teachers, administrators and textbook writers, a generous financial policy on the part of public authorities and business firms and recognition by the student of the need for intensive study, probably over a long period, these clearly must provide the basis for a valid approach to the problem.

The articles which we print on the use of the language laboratory, the teaching of languages by radio and television, the lessons to be drawn from general linguistics (P. D. Strevens), possible approaches for raising the standards of textbooks (P. D. Strevens as well as P. H. Hargreaves), furnish us with precise examples of the sort of thinking and experimentation which are going on at the present time, while J. Llasera's account of the Saint-Cloud method for teaching French to adults illustrates the kind of stimulus coming from abroad. In addition, most contributors

---

[1] For the best short discussion of the two approaches, see P. Newmark, 'Conflict in Teaching Methods', *Adult Education*, Vol. XXXIV, No. 5. January 1962, pp. 238–47.

touch inevitably on questions of method. Each writes as an individual, surveying his or her own particular field, commenting on aspects to be condemned or deplored on the one hand, recommended as successful on the other. In their references to issues such as the recruitment of native speakers as teachers (Jones and Hay; *passim*), the relative importance of grammatical correctness as opposed to spontaneity (Jones and Hay; E. Monkhouse), the value of the prose translation (O. Eisner; E. Monkhouse), the necessity for textbooks in advanced groups (Jones and Hay; E. Monkhouse), the use of descriptive phonetics (O. Eisner; E. Monkhouse; P. D. Strevens), their views may be to some extent controversial, since in almost all cases the problem has been thought out within the specific limits of the teaching of *adults*, reminding us that those who proclaim the ease with which youngsters absorb foreign languages are prone to forget how many different capacities may be called into play during the process loosely described as 'learning a language'.[1]

3. 'Vocational' and 'Non-vocational'

Thus, with regard both to methods and to aims, it is the complexity of the problem of how to teach a foreign language to the mature student which consistently emerges as the dominant theme of the collection, confirming the unhelpfulness in many contexts of relative expressions such as 'a good grasp', 'a reasonable standard', even 'a basic minimum'. For if it is difficult to specify where the learning of a language is to begin, who can say where it ends ?

In this respect one of the most interesting points to emerge from the symposium is that a desire to experiment, coupled with dissatisfaction at the *status quo*, are not only characteristic of

---

[1] An interesting article on this subject—Elisabeth Ingram, 'Age and Language Learning'—appears in our companion volume *Advances in the Teaching of Modern Languages*, ed. B. Libbish. Pergamon Press, 1964, pp. 18–24.

teachers charged with rehearsing pattern drills at speed for the benefit of business men, tourists and scientists but also of those whose concern it is to teach the foreign language as the embodiment of a foreign culture. Except where very short intensive courses with limited aims are in question, the distinction between the two kinds of teaching—'language' on the one hand and 'literature' or 'civilization' on the other—is in any case arbitrary, particularly when a certain level of knowledge has been attained, while in this country the issue is further complicated by the official classification of all education for adults as either 'vocational' or 'non-vocational', two categories which seem largely meaningless in the language field, convenient though they are for administrators seeking to decide upon rates of remuneration. The article which we include on current work at the City Literary Institute in London, a local authority institution (albeit of an unusual kind) where there is rebellion against the assumption that 'language' should be taught as though it were a simple 'skill', together with Dr. Monkhouse's inspiring account of her experiment for supplementing literature classes with instruction in language (carried out under the auspices of a university extramural department, naturally enough the arch-demesne of 'non-vocational' work), provide two examples of erosion of these artificial dykes which should offer encouragement to others elsewhere. Nor must it be thought that the drive towards more concentration on spoken contemporary usage is in conflict with this wish to deepen and enrich the teaching of modern languages; on the contrary, as our contributors make clear, the two are closely connected. Both are aspects of the weaning-away of language teaching from an excessive attachment to unquestioning routine, while the liberal values traditionally associated with the discipline of language study, far from being swamped by more 'practical' attitudes, are, if our contributors are anything to go by, being integrated into the teaching of languages to adults outside the universities as never before.

Commentary on the unreality of the categories into which language teaching to adults is divided under our present system seems to be provided by the relative similarity in the methods formerly found successful by Dr. Eisner, when working with evening students at provincial institutes of further education, and those described by Dr. Monkhouse in her extramural experiment in London. Like the account of work in the City Literary Institute, both affirm the essentially educative quality of the study of a modern language, the peculiar awakening of a sense of personal discovery that it induces and of which something is perhaps half suspected by the many adults who come flocking each October to languages classes with no very clear notion of why. All three articles certainly underline the high degree of linguistic attainment which a good tutor to adult students must possess, leading one to question whether our university modern language departments, who conduct so much of their work in English and whose products are already under fire for their inadequacy in the schools, could ever, without further training, satisfy the demands of the adult field. Even now it is usually taken for granted that organizers will go in search of native speakers, sometimes regardless of other deficiencies as tutors which they may well possess.

It must also not be imagined that those who work with the new media are remote from a view of language study as something more than the acquisition of a skill, as may be seen both from Miss Rowntree's interesting defence of—at the very least—her advanced radio courses against the charge of being too 'literary' ('we need the bricks as well as the tools of a language') and from Miss Sculthorp's comprehensive list of recommendations for the library of tapes which should be available in a language laboratory. In devising a new approach to language teaching for adults which is to satisfy all aspects of the national demand, the temptation to place too much emphasis upon the need for intensive courses with limited aims must perhaps be resisted, essential though these undoubtedly are at the moment to certain sections of the community. Once their immediate purpose is served, they will, one divines, go the way of so many other 'solutions' to the language problem, at least in so far as the European languages are concerned. Those who have faced a class of business men, engineers, scientists, ostensibly wishing to acquire a limited repertoire of useful phrases, know how soon many of them break through (and is this not legitimate and inevitable?) to a desire for wider linguistic horizons.

4. Who are the Students?

One of the difficulties in the way of framing a comprehensive estimate of the national demand has been that teachers and organizers, confronted with troops of students increasing yearly, have known very little about them, their background or their motives. Recent surveys now place at our disposal a certain amount of information which, while containing little to compel our surprise, nevertheless furnish us with some guidance.

The surveys in question were carried out (a) in close collaboration with the Principal and language staff of the City Literary Institute in London (one of the largest centres in the country, where every year some 2000 privileged adults receive 'non-vocational' linguistic enlightenment while many less fortunate are turned away), and (b) as part of a comprehensive study of all the evening centres in the city of Leeds.

The material on the City Literary Institute forms part of an investigation into the national provision for adult education in England and Wales which J. Lowe was able to carry out in the Extramural Department of Liverpool University through the generosity of the Nuffield Foundation 1961–63. The information concerning classes in Leeds has been made available to us by Mr. Ian Hanna of the Department of Adult Education, University of Leeds.

The first and salutary fact to emerge from our sets of figures is that great though the boom in language classes has been since the last war, it has been no greater than the general increase in demand for adult education of all kinds. At the Swarthmore Adult Education Centre in Leeds, for example, the increase in language classes has corresponded almost exactly with the increase in others. Let tutors and organizers in the modern language field hesitate, then, before considering themselves the special case which urgent demands from industry and other quarters may have led them to believe. On the other hand, our pilot study of the characteristics of those who come seeking instruction in foreign languages suggests that they do in fact differ to some extent from the general run of adult students.

Thus, in both places, language students do not turn out to be younger, as expanding tourism and talk of 'new attitudes' might lead us to expect, but older than adult students as a whole. They also belong to a higher economic social group. In the London figures, 11% more language students than any others belonged to the two socio-economic groups graded highest in the national census returns, that is to say to the professions and to administration and management, 5% fewer belonged to clerical grades, the number of skilled workers was also lower by 5%. A similar situation was found in the Leeds evening institutes, where language classes attracted practically no manual workers.

Another aspect of the same characteristic is that language students are drawn from the better-educated sections of society. In Leeds, for instance, where the evening institute population in general is weighted to the lowest end of the educational scale— that is to those who left school at fifteen or earlier—language students come mostly from the middle and upper end of the scale.[1] At the City Literary Institute fewer than one in ten seemed to have finished their full-time education in a secondary modern or elementary school, an average of three out of every five would seem to have left school after taking GCE 'A' level or its equivalent and two of these had a university degree, teacher's training certificate or comparable professional qualification. By comparison with the students in the Institute as a whole, 7%

[1] Care should be taken in interpreting this as an indication of *interest* in foreign languages. Only 12% of the listeners to the first Russian beginner's course put out by the BBC had left school at fifteen or before, but there is reason to believe that this particular radio audience is expanding. (See Miss Rowntree, who suggests self-consciousness as a reason for their preference for learning at home.)

fewer had left school at fifteen or under and 4% more had completed their education at twenty or over.

Lest these figures should be thought exceptional, dependent upon special circumstances in Leeds or a product of the high standards and social cachet attaching to the name of the City Literary Institute, it so happens that confirmation that they may be taken seriously as indications of the situation is available to us in the form of more general averages. Interrogation of adults studying all the non-vocational subjects offered to them at twelve centres spread throughout the country[1] revealed that it was the study of foreign languages and literature which attracted the highest proportion of people whose full-time education had continued until they were twenty or older. The figure was 42%, as compared with 31% *English language and literature*, 37% *philosophy and religion*, 37% *physical science*, 35% *archaeology*, and so on. At the same time only one subject had a lower percentage of students who had finished their education at fifteen or younger, namely *music* (14% as against 16%).[2]

---

[1] Details may be found in J. Lowe's full report of his pilot-survey, to be published in 1965.

[2] It should perhaps be repeated that the national figure quoted here is based on centres designated as specifically 'non-vocational' by the Ministry, that is to say, centres of 'adult' as opposed to 'further' education. Inclusion of figures for 'vocational' institutes (colleges of commerce and technical colleges), which also cater for thousands of part-time language students annually, would make some difference to the percentages. Whether the difference would prove particularly significant seems questionable. Truly vocational language work in institutes of further education constitutes an extremely small proportion of the part-time work as a whole. (See both our contributors in this field—P. H. Hargreaves and O. Eisner.) Teaching methods used successfully by the best tutors in both types of establishment appear similar and there seems room for doubt as to whether the type of adult who comes seeking language instruction of a general nature varies radically with the type of establishment he happens to pick upon. 'Examinations' are in evidence in vocational institutions, it is true, but only a handful of students have come specifically in search of them (GCE 'A' level, External London BA, Fellowship of the Institute of Linguists, RSA) almost certainly fewer people altogether than in one first-year class in Italian. Others accept good-naturedly the examinations that are thrust upon them or more often take advantage, equally cheerfully, of the fact that they are voluntary. (For comments on the use of examinations for administrative reasons quite unconnected

These facts surely offer a certain amount of directional guidance to planners of courses. One useful practical deduction, for instance, would appear to be that students who have never received at least some small degree of instruction in a foreign language will be very much in the minority. An extension of this certainly seems to be that almost all students will at some time have learnt a little French, however much they may clamour, out of a lack of confidence and because of unfortunate experiences abroad, to be admitted into beginners' classes. (This is, in fact, a well-known complaint among teachers of French to adults.) A new conception of the first-year course for adults in the French language as opposed to any other would seem not illogical, together with a new kind of textbook.

The popular image of adult education as the preserve of females, usually middle-aged, was seen from J. Lowe's averages to apply to language students as to others; 68% were women (cf. *English language and literature* 79% women). A close look at the detailed statistics for Leeds and the City Literary Institute is, however, more revealing. At the Institute, where the figure was thirteen females to every seven males, there were, even so, more males in foreign language classes than in any others. When it came to a choice between language and literature, substantially more men opted for language: seven of them to every five for

with the students themselves and the resultant pernicious effects on teaching methods in many classes, see P. H. Hargreaves, *Textbooks: the Present Situation*.) The experience of one of the editors when working concurrently in a university extramural department and with advanced classes in a large institute of further education also seems relevant. Only when the extramural lectures were delivered in the foreign language was there an appreciable difference in the kind of audience, which then (a further commentary on its 'non-vocational' appeal) often consisted of practising teachers of the language some of whom, perfectly reasonably, hoped to keep in touch with recent developments. In any case, the institute of further education offered a similar series of lectures each session—also in various foreign languages and also attended by teachers. That one (vocational) was to be regarded as markedly inferior to the other (non-vocational) was borne in upon the lecturer happening to deliver both by a certain difference in levels of payment. For this or some other reason, sixth-formers, excluded from the extramural provision, were also allowed to attend.

literature. Both these facts must, one assumes, reflect the practical career value of a knowledge of languages, calculated to attract men who would otherwise possibly not be interested in adult education. This seems to be borne out by the situation in Leeds where, astonishingly enough, men and women were almost equal in numbers in language classes as a whole, apparently because of the presence in curricula of certain specific courses designed to supply the needs of a number of men. Not only when tuition is laid on in collaboration with industry and commerce, but also in classes for languages such as Russian or Chinese, men are usually predominant. Thus, in a Russian course at the 'non-vocational' Swarthmore centre, two-fifths said that the subject would help with their jobs and in the whole of Leeds one-fifth gave the same reason for attendance at language classes in general. This may not seem a very high proportion until it is seen alongside J. Lowe's national average which is, in fact, only seven students out of every hundred. (The figure for the City Literary Institute was eleven.)

The typical adult student of foreign languages seems, then, to be emerging as not in the first flush of youth, reasonably well placed in society, educated above the average and, more often than not, female. When men equal or outnumber women there is a practical or financial explanation.

How does the figure of 7% having a clear vocational motive compare with other forms of adult education ? It is high, equalled in this investigation by the physical sciences only, where, incidentally, men for once outnumbered women and by as many as three to one. Other percentages were: *English language and literature* 3; *philosophy* 1; *psychology* 6; *archaeology* none. As for the motivation of the remaining ninety-three out of every hundred language students, the really valuable fact from our point of view is that whereas slightly less than a third expressed a special interest in language as such (contrast 74% for *general history*, 57% for *music*; compare 32% for *philosophy*, 29% for the *physical sciences*), almost all others—that is well over half the total number of students—gave their reason for frequenting language classes as a general desire to extend their personal culture. The figure was, in fact, identical with that for *philosophy* (58) and close, once more, to the *physical sciences* (61).

Of course, too much must not be read into these figures, especially since the increasing appearance of business men and technologists in the field, while unlikely to make much difference to the present social and educational level of students, cannot fail to swell the total of those whose interest in foreign languages is primarily vocational. But that such specific requirements should be treated as exceptional and deserving of specialist emergency attention is confirmed. The demand from the great majority of students seems to be of a rather different nature, presenting no less stimulating and exacting a challenge, requiring an equivalent revision of methods and attitudes, and with potentialities for the fostering of a more international outlook that seem incalculable.

Some of the tables upon which these assessments of the situation are based seem worth including. Thus, for the City Literary Institute, whose special characteristics should, perhaps, be borne in mind:

(a) *Occupations of Language Students*

	Higher admin., pro-fessional etc.	Other admin., pro-fessional etc.	Clerical	Skilled	Shop-keepers and assistants	Un-skilled
Combined Language and Literature	21%	45%	26%	3%	1%	4%
Language	22%	44%	25%	3%	2%	3%
Literature	17%	50%	26%	3%	0%	4%

(b) *Age on Completing Full-time Education*

	15	16	17	18	19	20 or over
Combined Language and Literature	9%	14%	16%	16%	7%	38%
Language	10%	15%	14%	17%	7%	37%
Literature	8%	10%	19%	15%	7%	41%

(c) *Motivation of Language Students*

	Language and literature combined	Language	Literature
General interest in continuing their education	44%	41%	50%
Special interest	42%	42%	39%
Social reasons	1%	1%	1%
To help in the service of others	1%	1%	0%
Primarily Vocational Motive	11%	12%	7%
No particular motive	0%	7%	3%

The striking fact here, as compared with other centres, is that such a high percentage should have declared a special interest in the subject as such. For liberal adult education students the percentage showing a vocational motive is also unusually high, in spite of the Institute's marked non-vocational bias. That a 'liberal' approach does not detract from a reputation for high linguistic standards would seem a valid and satisfying deduction.

5. The Future

If the picture built up by our contributors provides illustrations of how, in some quarters, problems of method are being identified and confronted with imagination, it also tells a tale of confusion and frustration in others, of administrative illogicality officially justified by parsimony, of hard-pressed trained teachers, native speakers whose potential value is largely wasted, staunchly philistine technical and commercial departments, alleged high aims that no one in the present circumstances expects to attain, submission to the dead hand of undistinguished examination programmes, and an absence of overall direction.

'The teaching of foreign languages to adults is a national problem, not a local one. Yet it is the job of no single person or institution to see it in national terms', says P. D. Strevens, while O. Eisner, dealing with vocational training, gives the English syllabus of the *Dolmetscher-Schule* in Munich to add precision to his own plea for something approaching a national language institute. Three recent reports—the Hayter Report on Oriental, Slavonic, East European and African Studies, 1961; the report of the Federation of British Industries on Foreign Languages in Industry, 1962; and the Annan Report on the Teaching of Russian, 1962—have all made reference to this gap in our education system; it is therefore hardly surprising to find that the lack of some organization,[1] which shall be at the same time a forum of opinion and a source of special training, is at least implicit in the conclusions of most of our contributors. Thus—with reference to textbooks—'There is unfortunately no common meeting ground for administrators, teachers, students, examin-

[1] As we go to press, we hear of the formation of the *Committee on Research and Development in Modern Languages*. The suggestions which follow are respectfully offered for its consideration.

ing bodies and publishers', says P. H. Hargreaves, while Miss Sculthorp, speaking of audio-visual aids, asks: 'Shall we in a few years' time look around at language laboratories fallen into disuse or disrepute? ... there should be more chance for practising teachers to be able to observe each other's methods in action if they so wish, and to be able to meet regularly to exchange ideas and discuss points in a way that would be much more practically useful than in association meetings.' The Army complains that there are no proper national training facilities for interpreters, and industry that there is no nationally recognized qualification for linguists. The City Literary Institute ponders the question of finding appropriate staff for advanced, non-vocational courses— 'where, at the present moment, can a prospective tutor gain the experience or training necessary for this particular branch of adult teaching?'—and at the university extramural level Dr. Monkhouse comments: 'The acquisition of the vocabulary associated with the contemporary scene leads at once to some questioning of the social and political assumptions which underlie it. . . . It must be admitted that it is hard to find tutors equipped to deal with this part of the syllabus. . . .'

At the present time the related questions of training teachers specifically for adult education, inquiring into community needs and attracting into the field graduates of the right quality, call for careful study. The universities have a vital part to play in this sphere of education as in any other, and it is encouraging to note that at least some of the new universities seem to be of this persuasion where modern languages are concerned. The institution of *a common training ground for all branches of adult language work* would raise standards; it would also produce a healthier situation from a number of points of view. Not the least saddening feature of the scene outlined here is that the present administrative fragmentation obscures the essential unity of the field of language teaching to adults, even for those who work within it, leading inevitably to underestimation of the difficulties posed by certain tasks, as well as of the interest and stimulus which each fresh demand can provide. The freelance teacher, native speaker or otherwise, called upon to fill (however inadequately) a succession of assorted and hitherto unsuspected gaps in various programmes and institutions, is perhaps uniquely placed to appreciate the general situation, but whether the present reliance upon such instruction should persist is a further question. It is no doubt true that adult education must always lean to some extent upon the part-time services of experts whose experience in the world outside institutions of learning forms a basic ingredient of their value as teachers. Yet, in reading the articles which we print here, it is difficult to avoid the conclusion that, where foreign languages are concerned, the overriding deficiency which characterizes all forms of teaching for adults lies in the staff, mostly part-time, which is at present available. For non-vocational as for vocational work, teachers of adults are *specialists*. They must speak the language well and they must be fitted to deal with more than those predominantly literary aspects of an alien civilization which receive emphasis during a university training, although, in view of the special characteristics of adult language students, few of us would claim, surely, that this foundation can be entirely dispensed with at any level? Whether, as things stand, plans for improving aims and results on a national scale could, in fact, be put into effect seems doubtful, unless help is forthcoming from a new class of professional tutors, who, among other things, shall have received an opportunity systematically to extend their knowledge of the social and political or economic aspects of the foreign country which is to be their special concern. That they should also have been able to observe the methods of tried teachers seems no less desirable.

If this symposium does no more than draw the attention of educationists and young language graduates to the size and the exciting nature of the problem of teaching foreign languages to adults in this country at the present time, together with the high calibre of the students who come forward, it will have fulfilled no small function.

MARGARET LOWE
JOHN LOWE

1 The Problem in Perspective

P. D. STREVENS

I

AMONG the long-term effects of the war, few people at that time would have anticipated a radical change in language teaching. In fact, a world-wide revolution was imminent in this field, but the causes of it—political, social, economic, military—were not yet apparent in Britain. Now, in the 1960's, the revolution is in full train; consequently, the task of describing the teaching of languages to adults in Britain is a complex one, partly because the position is still changing, but partly because the different sectors of the language teaching profession as a whole have become interdependent in new ways.

If the discussion of the teaching of foreign languages to adults is to be a meaningful and illuminating one it will be necessary first to see how the communication needs of Britain have changed in recent years; then to consider how the national provision of foreign language teaching is itself changing to meet the new situation; next, to look in some detail at the pattern of foreign language teaching in that area which dominates and determines all other areas (namely the teaching of languages in schools); and next to describe the new techniques and methods that are in use at all levels of language teaching. Then finally the present state of teaching foreign languages to adults in Britain can be seen in relation to the profession as a whole.

II

There was relatively little teaching of foreign languages to adults, pre-war. The Foreign Office and the Colonial Office had regular specialized needs for small numbers of officers, and

1

these needs were often met by the two great research institutions of the University of London, the School of Slavonic and East European Studies and the School of African and Oriental Studies, or by their counterparts in a few other universities. The extramural departments of many universities offered courses in some foreign languages, as did a few local education authorities. A very small number of commercial schools catered for the remaining adults who wished to learn foreign languages, perhaps to train as translators or interpeters, or to go as missionaries to far places. Language teaching was not big business in Britain before 1940.

This state of affairs was not surprising. The traditional British attitude was that foreigners should learn English rather than Englishmen learn languages, an attitude which seemed to be justified in practice. Because of Britain's political and economic dominance, those whose affairs brought them into contact with Britain used English.

Scientists were inclined to accept the view that everything of general importance and interest was accessible in English. The individual scientist was sometimes encouraged to learn to read papers in German, but British science and technology were, in general, unilingual.

The affairs of government, it is true, entailed contact with foreigners and occasionally the use of a small range of foreign languages, principally French and German. Among our diplomats and high civil servants there has long been a leavening of individuals with a brilliant practical command of French, of German or even of more exotic languages. But these have, for the most part, been isolated cases rather than large groups. Far more important has been the generalized understanding of the literature, culture and civilization of France and Germany which united the whole élite of government, regardless of individual specialization, an understanding shared by virtue of a common grounding in school French and school German.

Inter-governmental contacts were on a small scale, and international affairs were conducted by relatively few people, many of whom had only a reading command of a foreign language. This system worked tolerably well because the national communication needs were a matter of a small élite understanding and being informed about our neighbours, rather than a large number of individuals having a need for precise practical command of foreign languages.

In these circumstances the national provision of foreign language teaching was perhaps adequate, if not abundant. What did that provision amount to ? Instruction began in the grammar school and was supported by university courses in language and literature. Not all grammar school children learnt a modern foreign language, particularly if they went on to specialize in science subjects, but a good proportion of such children received at least four years of instruction in French or German. The pattern for preparatory and public schools was roughly similar, except that some preparatory schools started French earlier than the age of eleven, which was and still is the typical grammar school starting point.

The national needs for foreign language skills in the 1960's are of a different order and call for a different provision in the national education system. Trade and industry now have the most pressing reasons for making use of foreign languages, since their operations are more fiercely competitive with other countries and since the foreign customers and the overseas suppliers are nowadays quite liable to use their national language instead of English, and to prefer a firm which accepts this state of affairs to a firm which recognizes only English.

It is no longer possible for the scientist and the technologist to notice only what is published in English: he must be aware of specialist literature in other European languages, but above all in Russian, a language almost ignored in British language teaching before 1940. The launching of the first Russian sputnik in 1954 was an event of tremendous importance in the history of language teaching because of its effect in convincing scientists and governments that the individual scientist must be given access to work described in foreign languages. In the United States of America the reaction was immediate and dramatic: the National Defense

Education Act was passed, authorizing the expenditure of huge sums of money on the improvement of methods of language teaching and the provision of facilities for the teaching of languages. British reactions—the creation of the Association of Teachers of Russian in 1959, for example, and the Annan, Hayter and FBI reports—have been slower and on a smaller scale, but the intention is the same.

Government has become a complex affair, involving many more individuals in communication with foreigners than was previously the case. There has been growth of international agencies such as the United Nations, with UNESCO, WHO, FAO and the other organs of collaboration and technical aid; economic planning has linked us with Europe through the Council of Europe, the European Free Trade Area, Euratom and doubtless eventually the Common Market; military alliances such as NATO and its counterparts CENTO and SEATO repeat this pattern of international interdependence. But the important aspect of these developments, for our purposes, is that they have added to the national requirements significantly large numbers of individuals (probably several hundred extra per year) who now need to use foreign languages. Here, too, the trend continues.

Important though these developments are for national policy, pressure for foreign languages is being built up in yet another way, namely through the general expansion of international communication.

It is sometimes said that the English language is not really unknown to a Nigerian child when he first starts to learn it at school, because for the whole of his young life he has constantly been surrounded by advertisements, notices, broadcasts, films and even conversation in English. It is equally the case that the average Englishman or Scot nowadays meets a great deal of French, some German and a little Italian in his daily life. Films, radio and above all television, through the Eurovision link, combine to make life in Britain more cosmopolitan than it has been for centuries, and to make the notion of knowing foreign languages familiar and acceptable to the bulk of young people. This is a conditioning process, not a teaching process, but it contributes nonetheless to the language teaching revolution.

As the pattern of external pressures has changed in recent years, so it has suddenly become necessary to find many thousands of adults in Britain capable of making practical use of foreign languages. Here is the rub: the holders of the new jobs in industry and commerce, the outward-looking scientists, the new international administrators, the 'communicators' in the Service organizations, all need a type of practical ability in foreign languages—in particular, an ability to talk and write in direct communication with foreign counterparts, covering both everyday discourse and the specialized usage of their own jobs—which was not an essential feature of the language-learning received at school by pre-war generations of British children. This is the essence of the crisis in foreign language teaching to adults in Britain in the 1960's: the national needs are not only suddenly and dramatically greater in quantity, they are also radically different in kind. If the school system is not producing the people required in sufficient numbers, then adults must be given specialized training in languages at short notice, under emergency conditions.

III

The eventual solution of Britain's crisis in teaching foreign languages to adults may lie in the current wave of enthusiasm for teaching foreign languages in the primary schools. The paradox is not as great as might first appear, since in both cases the aim is to impart practical language ability, rather than the wider literary and cultural studies with which the universities (and, by reflection, the grammar schools) have traditionally been concerned. Nor does hope spring simply from the fact that the aim of the teaching is practical ability. The most important and suggestive feature of primary school language teaching is that it can be given to the whole range of children, not solely to those who will eventually reach the grammar school; this will assure that the sheer numbers of workers will be found since the base of the pyramid will be greatly broadened, and it also means that the pattern of secondary school language teaching can be—indeed, must be—totally revised.

Whereas in the past the grammar schools have been teaching children who have no previous knowledge of a foreign language, in the future, if the primary schools adopt language teaching as a normal feature of their syllabus, the grammar schools will have a task of keeping up, extending and building upon existing skills, instead of beginning from nothing. An additional foreign language would seem all the easier to add in the course of a grammar school education.

Similarly, secondary modern and technical schools would receive their pupils already able to use a foreign language. At last one could reasonably hope that young people going into office work, or dressmaking, or vehicle maintenance, might be able to make use of French books on cuisine or a Vogue dress pattern, or the maker's original handbook for a Mercedes-Benz, or even be able to type in French or German.

A painful road must be travelled before the first enthusiasm for foreign language teaching in primary schools can be canonized into becoming a regular part of their work, but there seems no reason to doubt that it will eventually come to pass. It seems firmly established that children learn languages more easily when young; that differences of intelligence (as distinct from personality) are relatively unimportant for this purpose; that excellent teaching can be done without the need for the teacher to have taken a university degree in the language and literature concerned. What is needed is a period of consolidation and reorganization to enable teaching materials to be prepared and to permit the teaching profession to organize into the training of primary teachers this additional skill. When all this has taken place the school-leaving population will come much closer to meeting the need for adults with practical language ability than is the case in 1964. In the meantime emergency measures are needed, to deal directly with adults, using the latest methods and techniques of language teaching.

IV

The main features of modern foreign language teaching for adults may be summarized thus:

A – Leads to practical language ability.

B – Concentrates on the spoken language, at least at the outset.

C – Produces specialized teaching materials for every different course.

D – Applies the products of modern linguistic science to the preparation of courses.

E – Teaches language in situations.

F – Teaches intensively.

G – Uses all appropriate teaching aids, especially audio-visual aids.

H – Avoids unnecessary teaching *about* the language.

Many of these are general principles which apply to the teaching of foreign languages in general, and each needs a word of comment.

A – If we restrict the discussion to adults outside the school and university system we see that much foreign language teaching leads to a well-specified end, is concerned with practical language ability and is in some sense vocational. There is, for instance, the course designed to equip an oil-drilling engineer to deal with an Arabic-speaking crew; or to enable a tea-planter to communicate with his foremen; or to permit an electronics engineer to talk to his opposite numbers on an airfield in Indonesia or Greenland or Peru; or to help a sales manager to set up a new office in an overseas territory. There are two important points here: first, this is usually language learning for the purpose of understanding a language as it is spoken and then speaking it before reading and writing it; secondly, the concept of 'learning Swahili' or 'learning

Malay', or even 'learning French', is rapidly being superseded by more specific aims, like 'learning Swahili to become an agricultural adviser', or 'learning Malay to become a road-planning engineer', or 'learning French to be an economist with the Council of Europe'.

B – Although a much more sophisticated analysis of language behaviour can be made, and is indeed sometimes essential in planning language materials, the gross labelling of the four 'basic skills' is widely accepted. Understanding speech, speaking, reading, writing: two skills associated with the spoken language and two with the written language. Each pair of skills comprises one that is predominantly *passive* (or 'receptive')—understanding speech and reading—the other largely active (or 'productive')—speaking and writing. There is general agreement that the passive skill should precede the active, within each pair, and that the command of the spoken language should precede the written. Here the definition of 'command' becomes crucial, and it is fair to say that opinions vary. Some authorities maintain a period of up to 60 or 100 hours of purely oral teaching before any teaching of reading in the foreign language is attempted; others hold that literate adults, particularly if they are well educated, linguistically sophisticated (in the sense of having previously studied foreign languages) and having a writing system running in the same direction as in the language being taught, may be introduced to written forms within a very few hours. Nevertheless, there remain two points which are widely agreed. First, if adult learners can become familiar with the sound of a language, and are able to make a tolerable imitation of what it sounds like before they first see it written, they may well have many fewer problems of spelling and orthography. Secondly, except in the rarest of cases the notion that a 'reading knowledge' of a language can be taught more quickly by going straight to the written language turns out to be a chimera. A reading knowledge *can* be taught in this way, but there is no evidence that teaching it thus is more rapid or effective, and a strong body of opinion exists which says that even if the spoken language is quickly abandoned, it is highly desirable to have passed through an 'oral-only' stage, and then subsequently made the conversion from spoken to written.

C – The next feature of modern language teaching is of crucial importance and affects the task in every detail.

It is not enough to specify in greater detail the aims and purposes of the course: in addition, the syllabus, textbooks, aids, which are normally subsumed under the label 'teaching materials', must be designed to lead to this particular end. The axiom of modern methods of language teaching is that ideally, every different language teaching situation requires its own specific teaching materials. This is partly a matter of suiting the content of the teaching to the purposes of the learner, so that the oil-well engineer applying himself to Indonesian learns to talk in fact about oil-wells and does not waste scarce learning time in mastering irrelevant language material. But there is much more to the method than mere vocabulary selection. Grammatical patterns need also to be selected on the grounds of their relevance to the precise purposes of the course. Even the sound-systems should be treated in the same way, so that the accent taught is appropriate to the circumstances in which the language will be used.

But it is not only the language content that needs to be adapted to the precise needs of the learners. The methods and techniques of presentation, too, are affected by a wide range of factors, including at least the following, and frequently several others:

SOME FACTORS TO BE TAKEN INTO ACCOUNT IN DESIGNING A
FOREIGN LANGUAGE COURSE FOR ADULTS:

1. *Aims and purposes of the course*
These have been discussed above. Their main effect is to determine the language content of the course, which is then treated in ways which will be described below.

2. *Average age of pupils*
The label 'adult' needs further amplification, if it can be

given, since a class of age eighteen will react best to different materials from a class of age forty.

3. *Size of class*

Methods of presentation and teaching that can be employed in a class of ten are often out of place in a class of fifty. The rule is clear: for teaching the spoken language, the smallest possible size of class is to be preferred.

4. *Previous language-learning experience*

The linguistically sophisticated adult who has previously studied two or more foreign languages is a pupil for whom almost all rules can be broken. The adult with little or no previous experience of learning a language often expects it to be a difficult task, which in consequence it then becomes. The learner's 'set' towards language learning is an important point to be studied.

5. *Average educational level*

It is not simply the intellectual calibre of the learners that counts, but also the kind and extent of learning that they are accustomed to, and how long it is since they last received any systematic teaching. The recent graduate is at an advantage over the more mature student simply because he is still in the habit of learning (or at least of being taught); but in addition a different approach might be needed for a class of a given average age whose members left school at fifteen, and a class of similar age whose members continued their education to twenty-three or twenty-four.

6. *Previous experience of the language being learned*

A course for beginners is different from a remedial or refresher course. (The French authorities responsible for the audio-visual course *Voix et Images de France* have always been insistent that only adults and only beginners should be taught by this course, since other categories of learners have difficulties that the course was not designed to meet.)

7. *Intensity of the course*

This is discussed in greater detail below. Clearly the shape of any course is vitally affected by the rate at which the teaching takes place.

8. *Proficiency of the teacher*

It is sometimes necessary to prepare 'teacher-proof' materials if it is known in advance that the proficiency of the teacher is not going to be up to the optimum required. There is no doubt that this can be done, but writing into the materials an insurance against inadequate teachers is likely to involve sacrificing other advantages. There is one absolute maxim: the teacher should always be familiar with the course he is using.

9. *Equipment available*

Teaching aids such as the tape-recorder and the language laboratory only reach their full potential if their use is integrated into a course when the course itself is being planned. They are best used not as occasional, extempore additions to the course but as deliberate, functional elements of it. Hence the need to know in advance what aids are available. The matter is discussed in more detail below.

10. *Motivation of the pupils*

A crucial question is: is it worth the pupil's while for him to succeed in the course? If it is, then he is likely to work well and assiduously, and to learn more rapidly and effectively. But an adult who is in the class 'because they sent me', and who wishes he were elsewhere, is likely to do badly.

11. *The pupil's mother tongue*

The difficulties and errors of any adult learner are largely determined by the nature of his mother tongue and by the similarities and differences that exist between his mother tongue and the foreign language he is learning. A teaching course should pay more attention to the areas of difficulty,

B

and less to those parts of a course which are learned more easily.

12. *Target standards*

A course must aim at a particular level of proficiency by the end of the course. It is difficult enough to specify language proficiency in any detailed and meaningful way; it is even more difficult to determine whether a given pupil has reached the required standard. Language testing is still in its infancy. Of foreign language examinations currently sat by school children and adults, hardly any produce a valid or reliable measure of overall proficiency in the basic language skills of understanding speech, speaking, reading and writing. The job of assessment is now a practical possibility and several schemes for the revision and development of tests and examinations are under way, but it will be a considerable time before a sufficient number of suitable tests and examinations are available.

There are, of course, very many other factors at work in determining the most appropriate teaching materials for any particular group of learners, but the foregoing is a selection of the most important factors, to which must be added one of the most vital of all, namely the application of linguistics to the organization of the language content.

D – Language teaching is not the same thing as linguistics, and their aims are different. The specialist in descriptive linguistics cannot do the job of the language teacher, nor can the language teacher expect to teach linguistics. But the task of imparting language skills is fundamentally regulated by what language is like. Any major development in our understanding of the nature of language, or of our techniques for describing particular languages, is likely to illuminate the task of the language teacher, and that is indeed what has occurred during the past few years.

The contribution of linguistics has been of two main kinds: first, in producing better descriptions of the languages being taught together with useful comparisons between the mother tongue and the language being taught; and, secondly, in providing a framework of organization for the language teaching items in a given course. The former contribution is fairly obvious: descriptions (especially at the level of grammar) of foreign languages have been less than perfect. They have sometimes included forms of the language which are 'schoolroom language' rather than valid current usage; they have often omitted large areas of the language which the learner needs to be taught. In particular they have often largely ignored the spoken language, or have assumed that it would be dealt with as a separate task in books on phonetics or pronunciation. Nevertheless, the improvements to be gained from better descriptive linguistics are of a more obvious kind than those which follow from better organizing the language items that are to be taught.

The 'language items' are the complete list of 'points to be taught' which every teacher and course designer and textbook writer begins with. (Language is, of course, much more than a collection of items, but the teaching process requires the total task to be broken down and described as if it were a large number of separate teaching items.) Traditionally, the textbook writer has drawn up his list on the basis of personal experience as a teacher, or by taking over some other author's list and making additions or subtractions, or by some similar, impressionistic method.

The contribution of applied linguistics to this task is to provide a job-analysis in terms of language, and to enable a check-list to be drawn up which will dovetail the pedagogical into the linguistic. To begin with, the question is asked, which variety of language is to be taught? Is it to be present-day standard French, spoken and written? Or spoken and written Brazilian Portuguese? Or spoken Mandarin Chinese? An act of *selection* is implicit in every choice of a target for language teaching, and an understanding of the different varieties of each language and of the differences between them make the act of selection a deliberate one, and therefore subject to control.

But even when the variety of language has been selected it represents a much larger body of language than can possibly be included in our actual language course. If one is designing a course of Russian lasting 200 hours and has selected current educated Moscow Russian, spoken and written, as the target, it is still unrealistic to suppose that 'the whole of' current educated Moscow Russian can be imparted in that time. A further process of *restriction* is needed, in which a deliberate decision is made to restrict the items which one is going to teach, limiting oneself to those needed for a particular degree of formality (e.g. by ignoring all styles more formal or informal than the one that is chosen), and for a particular purpose (e.g. the Russian of electrical engineering, or rocket technology, or language teaching). Even when thus restricted it may still be necessary to impose an arbitrary limit on the total size of vocabulary and the total choice of grammatical constructions, and to set up criteria such as frequency of occurrence in Russian, or 'teachability', or teaching convenience, in order to include or exclude particular items.

These procedures, *selection* of a variety of the language and *restriction* to certain items from a particular professional register and style within that variety, are necessary steps in the task and they are made more effective by being based on certain aspects of linguistics. Once they have been carried out the course-designer is at last in possession of the inventory of items that are to be taught. He can say precisely which items are to be included in his course and he can list a good many items which are not, and further (which is both important and relatively rare) he can give a reason for the inclusion and the exclusion of every item. He may say, for instance, as the authors of *Voix et Images de France* said, that the past subjunctive forms of French (*que je passasse*, etc.) are so rare in modern spoken French that they are omitted from a basic course for adults which lasts only 120 hours.

However, even when the list of items is complete it still has to be organized in sequence, making a deliberate decision to teach this item before that, and to delay some other item until after the introduction of something else. If one can say, as a generalization, that the selection and restriction were based chiefly on linguistic categories, and if the actual teaching of the items is based chiefly on good pedagogical techniques, then the processes of *staging* and *grading* can be said to draw upon both.

Staging is relatively simple. It involves allocating the items to the major time-units of the course in each year, or each term, or each month, or each week, or each day, or each lesson, or each part of a lesson, according to the way in which the course and the timetable are designed. But this procedure must go hand in hand with grading, which decides on the sequence of items. Thus it is not only a matter of deciding that (for instance) lesson 17 shall contain three new vocabulary items, revision of personal pronouns, and practice of a couple of consonant clusters. And the decision about how they are taught, and even about whether they are taught overtly as vocabulary and grammar and phonetics or whether they are embedded in a form of teaching that does not speak *about* the language—this decision belongs to yet another procedure, that of *presentation*, not to the procedure of grading.

Grading is a complex task, requiring the balance of many criteria, some of which may often conflict with each other. One obvious criterion is frequency of occurrence: if it is observed that a particular item is very frequent in the kind of Russian that has been selected this is probably a good reason for introducing it early. But if it happens to contain a difficult consonant cluster or an unfamiliar feature such as palatalization this might make it desirable to hold the item back until slightly later, when palatalization has been introduced and practised. Another criterion is 'teachability': depending on the methods of classroom presentation that are used, some items are easier or more difficult than others to put across and so may need to be held back or brought forward in the grading. Yet another factor is that some items may be taught early because they are necessary operators for classroom use.

There is a particular instance of this in teaching English as a foreign language, where two schools of thought differ sharply in their grading of the questions as a point to be taught. Teaching

'Is he going?' is different in a number of important respects from teaching 'He is going'. But the give-and-take of classroom teaching is so vastly helped by an ability on the part of the learner to handle questions and answers that most British specialists introduce question forms fairly early, thereby using convenience of presentation as a criterion for advancing the grading of certain items. On the other hand, for some of those American workers who make use of transformation grammar, questions are a fundamentally different type of grammatical item from statements; they should therefore not be taught until control of 'kernel sentences' (i.e. roughly, positive statements and assertions) has been established. There is something to be said for both attitudes: but whatever decision is reached it should preferably be for a cogent reason, deliberately applied.

Selection and restriction of the language content, staging and grading of the items thus determined: these are two of the chief contributions of linguistics to modern thought in our field. But it must be noted that setting up a 'check-list' to unite all these procedures into a single framework or organization for language items reminds the user that each of the procedures described, together with those of actual presentation, must be carried out at all levels of language. That is to say, they must all include the sound-systems, the patterns of grammatical usage, the patterns of vocabulary (because there are patterns within vocabulary, and they are different patterns from those of grammar) and the patterns of situations. Table I shows a summary of the framework of organization of language teaching items.[1]

E – The notion of teaching language in *situations* is not a new one. It has been recurrent in the history of foreign language teaching, but it is at present in resurgence in British practice. It

---

[1] This approach (which is becoming known as 'methodics') owes much of its origin to W. M. Mackey, and its further sophistication to J. C. Catford and R. Mackin of the School of Applied Linguistics of the University of Edinburgh, to whom particular and personal acknowledgement is made even though the present paper shows some detailed differences from their formulation.

is necessary to be clear about what is meant by 'teaching in situations'. Above all, the phrase refers to three notions: first, that language ought to be meaningful whenever it is taught and drilled; secondly, that one part of meaning consists in the

TABLE I: A FRAMEWORK FOR THE ORGANIZATION OF LANGUAGE
TEACHING ITEMS

(After Catford and Mackin)

	SOUND-SYSTEM	GRAMMAR	VOCABU-LARY	SITUATIONS
SELECTION of a variety of the language				
RESTRICTION to a particular style and register within that variety				
STAGING into major time-chunks of the course				
GRADING into the most appropriate sequence				
PRESENTATION in the classroom, involving choice of techniques, aids, etc.				

particular circumstances in which one piece of language is used rather than another piece of language; and thirdly, that since language is a form of behaviour it is always desirable to relate language teaching to the kinds of situation in which particular kinds of language behaviour take place.

It is easy to see that with young children this suggests activity teaching. But for adults, too, many people consider it advisable to reinforce language learning by 'suiting the word to the action' whenever possible, and by always relating a pattern to the situations in which it is appropriate.

F – The *intensity* of language teaching courses for adults varies within very wide limits. Quite apart from the degree of concentration that may be applied by any given teacher (or learner), the term intensity is here used in a specialized way.

Four components interact to give a measure of intensity: the total duration of the course, the total number of hours of teaching in the class, the frequency of the classes and the length of each class. In other words, a 250-hour course lasting six months is a different proposition from a 120-hour course lasting three years. Broadly speaking, the greater the intensity of teaching, the more effective and rapid the learning. Maximum intensity should always be sought for adults. Indeed many authorities regard full-time language learning (i.e. maximum intensity, with minimum overall duration) as being the ideal treatment for adults. A commercial firm would often rather release a man for a full-time course of thirty hours a week for four weeks than two hours a week for a year. One important aspect of intensive teaching is that it offers many fewer opportunities for forgetting.

G – Without exception, all the sophisticated teaching aids can be a help in teaching languages to adults. They consist of at least the following: gramophone, tape-recorder, language laboratory, audio-visual presentation, filmstrip, sound-films, radio, television, teaching machines and programmed instruction. Of these, probably sound films have been the least satisfactory in the past because of the low standard of sound quality in average school classroom conditions. But competition from television has led to improvements, and the other aids are already extremely valuable for various aspects of language teaching work. The best courses are those that have integrated into their content teaching aids of a kind suitable to the particular learners they are aiming at. It is likely that within five years the use of audio-visual aids and language laboratories will be considered a normal part of language teaching even in Britain. Until that comes to pass, and in particular until a greater range of teaching materials becomes commercially available, teachers will be in the difficult position of being fairly certain that audio-visual techniques and language laboratories can make a really significant advance in the teaching of practical language skills, and yet of not having the equipment or the courses (or, worse still, of having the equipment but not having the courses) to try them out. Of course, even in 1964 it is not true that there are no materials whatever. Courses for teaching a wide range of languages to adults by audio-visual and language laboratory techniques do exist, though it is some-times difficult to find detailed information about them, they are often extremely expensive, and (as one would expect in the early days of new techniques) some of them are less than mediocre in quality. These techniques are undoubtedly going to continue accelerating the language teaching revolution and teachers should be given the time and opportunity to experiment with the use of every available example in order to learn how to do even better.

H – The last of the features of language teaching which has been selected for comment is that it avoids teaching *about* the language. The theory is simple: teaching about a language (e.g. teaching grammatical rules, or teaching formal statements about vocabulary, or phonetics) is no substitute for actual practical use of the language. Teaching about a language—being able to describe it—has a function, it is true, but it is a very special function and one that belongs only to an advanced level of instruction. However, in the case of adults it is necessary to distinguish carefully between those adult learners on the one hand who are sufficiently experienced and sophisticated in language to be able to go direct from the abstraction which is a grammatical statement to the practical use and application of it, and those adult learners on the other hand for whom the rule is a largely unusable piece of information about the language. Here the unfortunate teacher has to beware of accepting too readily the adult learner's own judgement of how sophisticated he is. Because a man asks to be told 'the grammar' of Russian, for instance, is not in itself a reason to take up his time with grammatical description. The request may reflect nothing more than a memory of the way in which he learned French or Latin at school and an assumption that what was done then represents the only proper way of teaching the language he is now learning. There needs to be a clear showing that the leap from abstraction to practical use can in fact be made by the learner before he is presented with any substantial quantity of statements *about* the language.

V

The teaching of foreign languages to adults is a national problem, not a local one. Yet it is the job of no single person or institution to see it in national terms, to plan ahead, to relate the problem to the teaching in schools.

Britain urgently needs a body whose responsibility it is to know what theories and methods and techniques of language teaching are being used everywhere in the world; to be abreast of research and development in languages, linguistics and language teaching, and to sponsor and finance similar work in this country; to ensure that courses, textbooks and materials of the necessary kinds are available for the kinds of teaching the country needs; to keep the members of the teaching profession informed about new techniques and ideas; to ensure that professional training (including in-service training) takes account of modern ideas; to provide a national focus for everything that affects language teaching, both for adults and for children; to co-ordinate demands with facilities, as for example in assisting industry to find means of teaching the large number of adults it suddenly wishes to use in the field of international trade and commerce.

Perhaps we now have such a body. Since November 1964 there has been in existence a National Committee for Research and Development in Modern Languages, whose terms of reference come close to describing the functions outlined in the previous paragraph.

The late Professor J. R. Firth, writing in 1937 (in the final paragraph of *The Tongues of Men*, re-published by Oxford University Press in 1964), saw the need for 'some national provision . . . for the more modern linguistic sciences, on a scale commensurate with the wealth and position of Britain and America'. In 1965 the need is even more urgent than it was twenty-seven years ago, and the new problems serve only to accentuate our need for specialist co-operation in the fields of linguistics, applied linguistics and language teaching; that is, for the creation of machinery that will guide and co-ordinate the whole national effort in language teaching.

2. The Language Laboratory

Mabel A. L. Sculthorp

As geographical barriers have become of little account in these days of easy travel and communications, there is a more general expectation that it should be possible for anyone wishing to do so to acquire a working knowledge of foreign languages. Through holidays abroad, the exchange of children with foreign families, the twinning of towns, through popular education in economic and trade questions, we understand that we are living on the fringe of a multilingual society and that if we confine ourselves to speaking English we are often at a loss and disadvantage, whereas if we reach a certain proficiency in other languages on the personal plane we can the more easily travel and get to know people, help ourselves and others when difficulties arise, exchange ideas of interest to us all, and on the professional plane we can the more easily transact business, talk science, technical matters, international affairs. From the wish to the achievement is but one easy step in the minds of optimists used to the promises of success held out by the publicity men with regard to many spheres of activity today.

Learn a new language the natural way ? In the learning of one's mother tongue many stages can be distinguished. The weeks-old baby has the sounds of human speech constantly drifting in through inattentive ears, and only by the biologically built-in nuisance-noise of wailing can he demand attention. As the months pass, he attaches significance to what he hears : the cooing tones are associated with smiling faces and pleasant consequences, the sharp tones accompany the cold expression and retribution— speech is received as part of behaviour, and understanding starts. The baby voice is consciously exercised in a great variety of noises, then the pleasure of mimicry and repetition is discovered and 'mummumma' and 'daddadda' are lent unintended meaning by the admiring parents, who then become patient and devoted language teachers. From the second year on, the infant acquires through listening experience, imitation and correction his own everyday structural use of language. School adds further dimensions to language learning: the acquisition of reading and writing skills, the study of syntax, literary appreciation. But while it would be facile to suggest that the learning of the first stages of a foreign language in school or later in life could be assimilated in a purely natural manner, it seems to many that the natural sequence and the natural principles of learning should be respected. And if indeed a main need is to be able to talk, it is common experience to observe that the intellectual exercises generally demanded by a grammar and translation technique applied too soon can inhibit the flow of speech that should make it possible to express thoughts spontaneously. It is no new notion to use an active oral approach for the teaching of a foreign language, and when this method is pursued it can prove lively and interesting to the students—although exhausting to the teacher—and provided that the structures of language are introduced and dealt with systematically and with discipline, as all good language teachers will ensure, this approach can lay a good foundation for the formal work at a later stage. It is to those primarily concerned about the living language of speech that the language laboratory holds out hope of help.

The rapid technical development of sound-recording during the 1940's was timely: there could have been no needs more convincing than those of war to urge the importance of language as communication, and the ability to register one's voice personally gave for the first time the possibility of practice-in-sound heard and judged objectively. The steps from sound-mirror to magnetic wire-recorder and magnetic tape-recorder were useful advances, but of equal usefulness was the ability to erase recordings at will. The development of the technical devices in the military organization at SHAPE brought the electronic engineers into contact with the linguists and language teachers there who had been quick to put the equipment into action for their own purposes. It was the collaboration of the two groups that led to the development of the twin-track tape-recording principle, so that on one track teaching material could be recorded and stored and played while on another track student oral responses could be made and examined and re-made on silent stretches of tape left between the listening assignments on the master track. Today reasonably priced twin-track tape-recorders are available to any student of foreign languages wishing to work on his own by listening and speaking, and the twin-track principle is still the basis of the equipment of many standard language laboratories used in this country.

The term 'language laboratory' is not a happy one, but was the one firmly established by usage in the United States before the French and then the British adopted their installations. Alternatives have been tried—'studio', 'workshop'—but these have not been accepted widely enough to replace a term with which few are satisfied. The interpretation of what equipment a language laboratory should contain and what work should be done there appears to differ widely. The language laboratory should not ideally be used as a general-purpose language room in which all such admirable language teaching aids as record-players, radio, television, filmstrip- and cine-projectors are used for group listening and viewing, but rather as the one place in which an economically desirable and educationally approved number of students can all work aloud simultaneously or where they can carry out individual aural/oral assignments or go for the listening equivalent of a library session. It is undesirable that the machines that give these special facilities should stand idle or be inaccessible for maintenance because ordinary teaching has to be carried out in the room, and it can be restricting of laboratory-use time also if the making of master recordings puts the room out of use for student work. As the installation includes fairly expensive recording equipment, it is important that the apparatus should be used fully in as effective a way as can be devised.

Essentially, a language laboratory provides the conditions for people to listen and speak and receive private tuition from the teacher without interference to or from their neighbours. Students sit separately at sound-proofed positions that offer an illusion of privacy; from a control console the teacher can monitor individual work without interrupting the worker, can enter into private two-way conversation with any student, can be summoned by anyone needing help or can address the whole group. Many experiments have been made to find the best seating arrangements, but preferences differ: some teachers and students wish to be able to see each other (although the glass fronts to the booths in some laboratories are used only so that students may see the front screen when visual material is used with the audio-work), while the extremist Japanese professor thought it desirable for a door and a ceiling to be added to the solid-sided student booth so that isolation should be complete. The amount of equipment at the disposal of the students can vary widely, and should be decided only after the examination of fundamental principles. What is the aim of the laboratory work to be? Will students be monitored, sometimes or always? Is it desirable that they should record themselves? Should they have full control over their own machines?

Work in the laboratory is intended to intensify language learning. In spite of most interesting and successful self-instruction language courses developed in the United States by Professor F. Rand Morton, it will be a long time before this treatment in isolation of a social skill is perfected and becomes widely adopted, but when that stage is reached this form of self-instruction might be the answer to the insuperable obstacles to language learning at present experienced by those whose circumstances make it genuinely impossible for them to fit in with other arrangements. Thus at present the language laboratory cannot be called a teaching machine—it can supplement the complete course given by a teacher, saving time and reinforcing learning and leading to more effective aural comprehension and a more competent speaking of the language. The student's progress through laboratory work depends on his ear, on his ability and readiness to be self-critical, and on his diligence. Fortunate students could therefore work on their own in the laboratory with good profit, but any who lack but one of the qualities need the help and training and spur that the teacher can provide through vigilant and sympathetic monitoring. Unmonitored work spells danger if mistakes are becoming ingrained for one reason or another, and since it is inevitable that a good proportion of every student's work in the laboratory will of mathematical necessity go unchecked, there are some authorities who claim that it is safer for students not to have recording facilities but instead to rely on their own instantaneous judgement of their performance as they hear it in audio-active headphones. Yet this is wasting the greatest potential self-help the adult student can have at his disposal. Better to perfect one's monitoring system and to learn more about the correction of the faulty ear (or temperament), it might be thought. It is possible to run a language laboratory entirely by remote control: the students would have only earphones with a boom microphone, their programmes would be put out from a central position, the teacher could record them at his console. To operate thus is undoubtedly to avoid maltreatment of equipment, but it seems to negate the personal responsibility wherein lies the chief attraction of the language laboratory techniques to the majority of adult learners. Given the full facilities to receive master programmes on their tapes, to listen, to respond, to record, to play back and evaluate, to erase and re-record, all at their own tempo, adults can derive the utmost benefit from their sessions in the laboratory.

First principles thought out, the main problem is to provide suitable master recordings for use in the laboratory. For beginners there is a great advantage in using an audio-visual course that satisfies one's own requirements. One will need to examine the interest content and the linguistic composition, one will need to understand and respect the intentions of the authors for the presentation and practice of the material. The European pioneers at the *Centre de Recherches et d'Études pour la Diffusion du Français* at Saint-Cloud, with recent collaboration from the university of Zagreb, now have introductory audio-visual courses in several languages to their credit. Filmstrips form the visual content—this still form of illustration can be clearly allied to the linguistic meaning, and the pictures are thus a helpful adjunct to the tape-recordings of dialogue. It is important to remember that with such a course the laboratory phase is only the middle one of a sequence of three: the presentation of the situation and putting over of the meaning by direct method is classroom preparation; the laboratory then affords the opportunity for the individual practice of the dialogue, when all can work intensively for a period and when memory-work can be tested; but this is merely a preparation for the ultimate stage of the active use of the acquired language material in free context, when the teacher conducts the social group. From American sources other courses are available, some using motion pictures as visual illustration of the spoken language, others being audio-lingual without visual aids. Many of these have been developed by very successful language teachers and certainly deserve respectful examination, especially those that have considerably extended pattern-drills and structure-drills and -tests, for these techniques have been experimented with in the United States for several years, whereas linguists in this country have given little lead in such work. Yet ultimately it would be regrettable if commercially available new-style language courses not perfectly suited to our own circumstances were adopted simply because they are there to hand and good language teachers have not sufficient knowledge to produce their own audio-lingual materials. It is encouraging that some experimentation is now going on, and it can be expected that good teachers of experience and young teachers recently trained to use new aids will develop suitable techniques for reinforcing aural comprehension and oral fluency without rejecting what has hitherto been successful in our traditional language teaching.

The production of tape-recordings for work in the language laboratory is circumscribed by the limits of what the equipment can offer and subject to the needs of the students. First, the equipment offers the opportunity to listen and to *hear*, the passive but contributory skill that is one side of the business of communication, and this exercise can be a useful one for beginners and advanced students alike. The first listening spells will attune the ear to the foreign language in action, and all subsequent spells will add to the student's experience. No longer is the student limited to hearing the foreign language as it is spoken by his teacher alone, for the resourceful teacher now has the ability to organize on tape other sources of language: the young foreign assistant employed at the school, others from the neighbouring schools, a colleague's foreign wife, visitors from abroad, friends and strangers abroad, foreign gramophone records and radio broadcasts—the professorial speech can be countered by the natural speech of everyday occasions, the richness of literary and rhetorical masterpieces can be the foil to the limited speech of ordinary conversation. And as perceptiveness of ear is vital to the improvement of one's own speech, ear-training through listening and aural tests can be as necessary in language work as in music, begun by contrastive studies in the sound of language and used in individual remedial exercises when personal deviations are noted later. Listening is a powerful aid to the memory also. Dialogue repeatedly heard becomes usefully stored away for future use, and sets of sentences using the same structure patterns can drive home points of syntax in a surer way than the premature learning of grammatical rules. Yet no one would advocate such learning outside the meaningful situation, so that the ensuring and testing of comprehension is always essential, still using as far as possible the foreign language as medium. The first putting over of meaning belongs to the pre-laboratory teaching phase and it should therefore be taken that the practice tapes used in the laboratory will present no unknown features of vocabulary or construction. Let the teacher of groups beyond the first stages where audio-visual courses can help look to the books he is using—provided he knows he has the best and most stimulating for his classes—and think out the transference of the printed reading matter on to tape. In some cases a straightforward reading by an appropriate voice will do something to enliven the

passage for the learner, or sometimes a narrative can be drama-
tized, or supplementary preparatory or follow-up material may
be devised, remembering that heard language can best be used to
accustom the ear to the stuff of natural speech or in the very
different function of aiding literary appreciation. For the bridg-
ing over from passive to active work in the laboratory the listen-
and-repeat exercise is the most obvious one, and can be made a
useful challenge at all stages of learning the language, provided
that it is always allied to a critical discrimination by the ear of the
working student.

But it is through exercises requiring adapted or composed
responses that the student's growing knowledge of usage can be
tested and that he can be given the preparation for the free use of
language. All teachers and students are familiar with the types of
exercises frequently met with at the end of the chapters in the
formal language course-books: some of these are translatable into
terms of tape-recordings, while others are most certainly not—in
any medium it would be best to drop the type of exercise sentence
that consists of dashes precariously strung together with a few
minor parts of speech, or sentences peppered with suggestions in
brackets (infinitives of verbs or even words in a different language). When recording exercises for individual oral work in the
laboratory there are special factors that the teacher needs to bear
in mind. The objective should be to extract correct spontaneous
answers from the student, so that adequate preparation should
cover new points before the practice and test phase, the purpose
of the exercise should be clearly defined and illustrated, and then
the student must be led by imitation, memory and analogy to
produce the answer. In each exercise, which will generally
consist of multiple examples of a similar pattern, the student
should be required to change only one element. Examples will
be given first to set the pattern of the exercise. Further sentences
will then be given one by one, each followed by a pause for the
student answer, and this will immediately be followed by a
recording of the correct version and a silence in which the working student can register a correction or repeat with better

fluency or more native intonation. Spontaneity will be encouraged if the pace set by the tape is lively, so that the student will not have the time to analyse. Each foreign language has its special features that will cause difficulty to the learner, and teachers must be prepared to give these points additional practice in the language laboratory. Highly inflected languages such as German and Russian demand a more lengthy and painstaking build-up of patterns than French and Spanish and Italian, all will need practice in the substitution of object pronouns for nouns, in tense manipulation and in the combining of sentences and the use of subordinate clauses. It is obviously an exercise of the teacher's skill to devise examples that are clear and will hold the student's interest, that will call forth one unequivocal response and arm the student with the indispensable elements he needs for talking and writing the foreign language.

The usefulness of the laboratory equipment is likely to end with the manipulation of language of the kind already outlined, for it cannot deal correctively with creative language practice. Questions to be answered will have to be framed in such a way as to have an obvious answer if a solution is to be offered. Question–answer sequences are not conversation, and that art will only begin to be developed in the personal situation outside the laboratory. If free responses are called for on tape, whether as multiple-possibility answers or as a form of free oral composition, or interpreting and oral translating, the only way of dealing with this work will be for the teacher to take the tapes away for individual examination, as there is never time in the laboratory period for more than a fraction of each student's work to receive close personal attention. Hence the need for corrections always to be given immediately following the student's attempt, and the absolute necessity for a careful training of the student's powers of self-criticism.

The main practical advantages in having a language laboratory are that one can greatly augment the time each student spends on oral work, and that the oral assignments can be made entirely individual. Thus each student can be actively and purposefully employed for the whole of the laboratory period, whereas in the classroom he may have only two or three minutes in which to try out his reading or speaking of the foreign language. And now in the laboratory he may be provided with a tape that is right for his own requirements: he may be making up a lesson missed through absence, or revising earlier points he failed to grasp; he may be lagging behind or forging ahead of the others in his group. To provide for different rates of working or for the necessity of exercises at different levels within the class the teacher will be well advised to organize tapes of graded sets of useful exercises of many kinds, all of which will call for testing answers, often oral, but which may require a written response to the aural presentation of material. Comprehension passages ranging from the short and simple to the long and difficult may be tested by spoken answers, but more subtle questions could require written answers to be handed in. At advanced stages students could work through sets of translations, orally with suggested versions recorded to correct by, or in writing to compare with a hand-out or to give in for correction. Sets of graded dictations with duplicated sheets available for self-correction afterwards would give additional practice to students preparing for examinations. Reading practice is dependent on the student's self-appraisal if it is to be helpful. The printed passage can be marked off in phrases and an exploded reading recorded on tape, then the exercise can be varied according to the student's need, the student recording either before or after the master voice, and judging his own performance. All these individual exercises can be given either as part of the language lesson or undertaken voluntarily by the student in laboratory study periods. Recordings should be available from the library of tapes that must be built up for the language laboratory—a library that will eventually include not only linguistic work-tapes but also recordings of radio broadcasts, performances of plays and readings of other literary works and tapes of opera, songs and other music forms, the study of which adds to the richness that belongs to an interest in a foreign country.

It must be apparent that a language laboratory entails what might be termed hidden work and hidden expense. In the early stages of language teaching in exchange for—but later in addition to—the arduous marking of written work, the teacher must now spend as much time as he is prepared to give to scripting, recording and stage-managing the recording of tapes in preparation for the laboratory periods, even though each assignment of laboratory practice for a forty-minute period will last no longer than some ten minutes. In the busy laboratory the question of organization is crucial. Teachers need equipment, time, place and perhaps assistance to make their recordings. Master recordings need to be ready when students walk into the laboratory. The equipment must be checked and maintained. When these processes are carried out the laboratory will be immobilized. Therefore, in order to make the best use of the laboratory, it is desirable to have additional recording facilities elsewhere, to have pre-recorded student tapes, and to have technical assistance available to the teaching staff. However reliable the equipment, however well organized the running of the laboratory, at one level there are many regular small attentions that it is unsuitable to have the academic staff spending time on, while at another level there are highly technical processes that the academic staff will probably be incapable of doing well.

During the last years news of modern materials and aids and techniques has been spreading rapidly, and there are now laboratories established up and down the country where visiting teachers can inform themselves and observe, so that fears about mechanical and personal inadequacies should no longer persist. It remains important, however, that before having to use a language laboratory teachers should understand the fundamental teaching principles involved and should have an interest in their use—in order truly to teach, the teacher must inspire confidence in his students. In the past, good teachers have taught foreign languages well without the benefit of special equipment, but with effective aids most teachers can be more stimulating, and there is a growing number of teachers today who thank the opportunities of the language laboratory for keener student attitudes and improved standards in the aural/oral skills, which are reflected in general language work also. Students most frequently enjoy their laboratory work, for they generally wish to be able to speak the language and they realize that they now have greatly increased opportunity to practise doing this. Adults in particular can be seen to respond well to the use of the machines. They appreciate the privacy in which they can make and get rid of their errors and overcome the self-consciousness that is so commonly a drag on speaking out in a foreign language, and it is noticeable that the confidence they build up in the laboratory carries over into the group session. Adults are glad to have the ability to recall the recordings at will and without embarrassment, and they find that the tireless repetition that the equipment allows is an aid to a memory no longer easy to impress. Adult students like to have the impression of independence of working and the responsibility for making progress, and modern pedagogy tries to use this attitude. The tape-recording equipment is helping language teachers to respect these feelings, and there are many who are hoping that, in addition to aiding people to learn, the equipment will ultimately be used as a teaching machine. This will mean the possibility of dispensing with the teacher in the preparation, practice and testing phases of the work. Before this possibility can be reached, however, the whole of the linguistic content of a language must be codified and one must be able to programme the entire instruction step by step. It could then be envisaged that people could bring themselves along in a language up to a certain point at which they would at last be obliged to use the language socially with at least one other person, whose unpredictability might be very disconcerting after the machine. Whatever method is in fact used for language teaching, this is the bridge that must ultimately be crossed.

In the light of recent trends the teacher's task needs to be reassessed. The autocrat was always specially out of place with adult students, but now the class has developed into a co-operative venture in a real sense. The teacher has needed help from linguistic advisers, he has had the assistance of native speakers for pre-recordings, he has had technical assistance in the language laboratory, his students take a greater part in working for themselves, and he himself is released from much of the repetitive work and can concentrate more on tutorial work with individuals and on the follow-up of the learning phase. Whatever one's methods of language teaching, there are certain criteria that can be observed in good classes. The ambiance will be encouraging—students will want to arrive on time and will at once enter an atmosphere created by a friendly teacher waiting to greet them and talk in the language they come to learn. Students will show initiative in speaking, the class will not be tied to a coursebook. These are features that a good teacher may achieve at an earlier stage thanks to modern linguistic materials and the well-planned use of a language laboratory. For the highly organized, mechanistic business of drills and repetitions is never considered as an end in itself but only as the sound foundation-laying for a new form of total behaviour, one aspect of which is the use of language to express oneself.

If there were to be discovered a discrepancy between the principles and the practice in the use of language laboratories this should cause no surprise to the cynic, and the sceptic is asked to remember that we are dealing with a medium that is still new to us. Until very recently teachers in this country have had to look abroad for advice, and all too few have had the opportunity to travel overseas to see materials and equipment in action with classes of a similar composition to their own. They have even found it difficult to trace and obtain books on the subject. Indeed, we are still almost entirely dependent on the USA for literature about the language laboratory. Elton Hocking, of Purdue University, can be considered the doyen of practitioners and a most wise counsellor, and Joseph C. Hutchinson, now at the US Defense Language Institute, is a pioneer of great good sense, and all our libraries should hold their writings and those of Nelson Brooks, Robert Lado, Fernand Marty, Edward M. Stack, to name but some of those with opinions well worth reading.

Yet the experience and guidance of these experts have not suf-
ficed to prevent the misuse of language laboratories as these have
multiplied in America in the last few years. We are now faced
with a similar rapid growth of installations in this country. Shall
we in a few years' time look around at language laboratories fallen
into disuse or disrepute ? Let us by all means try to ensure that
there is not an over-zealous expansion of language laboratories
before we know how to use them with profit, but let us not stifle
experimentation that has already captivated many people's
interest and may lead to time-saving and greater personal
proficiency. Knowledge about the technical specifications necessary for good reception and recording will doubtless be more
widespread, the dissemination of information on all aspects of
the subject should be facilitated, courses and periods of trial
practice should be more readily available. Above all, there should
be more chance for practising teachers to be able to observe each
other's methods in action if they so wish, and to be able to meet
regularly to exchange ideas and discuss points in a way that would
be much more practically useful than in association meetings. It
is not easy to find an escape from the exigencies of a teacher's
timetable, but new language laboratories are being installed
almost every month at present and it is in the national interest
that we should find out how to use them for the better teaching
of foreign languages. As far as our grammar schools and universities are concerned, we have an experience in language teaching
that must not be denigrated. Can we but take a sympathetic
interest in the personal and social language needs that are met
with in adult life, and adapt for them, the new aids will be in
good hands. Teachers of adults must drop the idea of the
mystique of language learning, they must not be tempted to
despise the unacademic, they must remember that through the
centuries there have been many thousands of British travellers,
missionaries, pioneers, business men who *have* learnt to use
foreign languages in order to win influence, and that therefore
our present aims are by no means as new as the aids that are
designed to bring about their realisation.

3. The Saint-Cloud Method

Presented by JEAN LLASERA from
reports published under the direction of MONSIEUR P. RIVENC

Introduction

The Saint-Cloud method is intended for adult students commencing the study of the French language; it is based on studies of fundamental French made under the direction of Professor Gougenheim and on teaching research carried out at the *Centre de Recherches et d'Études pour la Diffusion du Français* under the direction of Monsieur Paul Rivenc. Experiments in the use of cinema for the teaching of French are also taking place at Saint-Cloud.

I. Le Français Fondamental

Fundamental French (*le français fondamental*) came into being as the result of recommendations made by UNESCO in 1947, when a committee of linguists proposed the diffusion of civilized languages as one of the most useful ways of fighting the ignorance and poverty which are widespread throughout the world. By means of these languages it would be possible to propagate more widely the notions of hygiene, domestic economy and technology which could help these 'underdeveloped' peoples to improve their material conditions and to raise their intellectual level. Two categories of civilized languages were envisaged: on the one hand, regional or local languages which have become civilized languages, and, on the other, universally used languages such as French and English.

UNESCO's intentions were similar to the preoccupations of a number of modern nations, including France itself, which was particularly interested. These preoccupations are, first, to spread knowledge of the language in overseas territories; secondly, to teach the language to the greatest possible number of foreigners; and, thirdly, to teach it to immigrants coming to work in France.

Whilst the importance of French as a universal language remains an important factor, the chief consideration nowadays in every country is to make contact not only with the cultivated classes but also with the ordinary people. The high standard in the teaching of cultural subjects attained in French public and private establishments abroad scarcely meets the needs of the ordinary people, who attend evening classes and demand efficient tuition with quick reliable results.

Another illusion, which found a noble defender in the person of a member of the *Académie Française*, is that the beauty of the French language lies in its very difficulty. Students of French are to be told that the language may be compared to a complicated game abounding in special rules: this conception is both false and dangerous. It is false because these subtleties have merely been added by the grammarians of the eighteenth and nineteenth centuries and have no justification of any kind, for a language is not a game of bridge or football. The conception is also dangerous because it runs the risk of putting off a great number of people who would like to get to know the French language but who either do not have the time to learn these highly subtle rules of grammar or who, taking them for what they are worth, cannot resign themselves to making the considerable effort required to master them.

The conception at the origin of basic vocabularies, and more generally of basic languages, relies on the idea of *limitation* of vocabulary and grammar. Modern languages have immense vocabularies, enriched by many technical expressions and infinitely diversified by the complexities of modern civilization. How many words (not just technical terms) stay buried in dictionaries and are never spoken aloud! The cultivated person understands these expressions when he meets them in a particular text, and knows how to use them in a moment of learned refinement. The grammar of modern languages is both complex and subtle, containing many forms which writers themselves hesitate to use, as well as rules which have long since become out-of-date.

Fundamental French (*le français fondamental*) has been thought out according to a method which, it is believed, is the first step towards the technique of basic languages. It combines:

(a) the *frequency* of words in the *spoken* language;
(b) the most useful words available;
(c) words which are not often used, but which we must have at our disposal (chiefly concrete words).

The first part of Fundamental French (*le français fondamental, 1er degré*) created by the *Centre de Recherches et d'Études pour la Diffusion du Français* is based on a list of word frequencies of the spoken language calculated through the use of tape-recorders, and on research made into centres of interest concerning basic vocabulary.

II. The Method 'Voix et Images de France'

Theory of the Method

(1) *A realistic vocabulary and basic grammar*. The teaching of a language and the acquisition of vocabulary have for long been treated as almost one and the same thing. Too many authors have weighed down the first few hours of teaching a language with a great number of rarely used concrete words, which, though sometimes picturesque or learned, are of little practical use; these words are rarely studied later on, and the pupil can only remember them by their very strangeness. Learning a language does not mean collecting words or expressions denoting rarely used objects. Certain authors, guided by the desire to omit nothing, used to teach vocabulary by using successive centres of interest to introduce in a descriptive text thirty or forty nouns for the home, the human body, clothing and so on. This emphasis on description sometimes makes one forget that language is essen-

tially a means of communication between human beings or social groups, and that description is not therefore its principal function. At an early stage in the teaching of the language the student should be able to express himself on various subjects; it is not necessary for that purpose to teach him from the very beginning a great number of words, and certainly not descriptive concrete ones.

For this purpose a small number of carefully chosen concrete words can suffice to describe the background and characters of a story, and to give the circumstances of the action. The student's efforts must, in order to be useful, be guided towards a precise objective which is not too far distant in time. He must be taught what will be immediately useful to him, and this small amount of knowledge will prepare him for a large number of actual situations. There are words which are always in use and others which are quite rare. If the vocabulary given is to be used as rapidly as possible by the student it must not, in the first place, be given in too great a quantity; the student must be taught and made to use essential *fundamental* words and constructions. These essential ideas must, of course, be chosen methodically, and be based on a careful study of linguistic realities, thanks to research wide enough to provide sufficient control. The experience of one isolated teacher, or even of a small group of teachers, however rich, subtle or precise it may be, cannot suffice to make this choice. A useful vocabulary is in the first place both general and related, containing verbs, grammatical expressions, adjectives and adverbs, together with a certain number of indispensable basic words.

The authors of *Voix et Images de France* have kept very close to the basic list of Fundamental French (*le français fondamental*) and any changes have been made only after long and careful study. The student can therefore assimilate in the first part of the course a vocabulary of approximately 1500 words, which will permit him to express in a correct and even amusing fashion most aspects of the activities of everyday life.

The continuation of the course will provide a richer vocabulary, at once more abstract and more subtle: it will be based on Fundamental French (*le français fondamental, 2ème degré*), which has recently been produced as the result of research made into the written language. Later on, further lessons will initiate the student into the language of art and literature and the specialized vocabulary of science and technology.

(2) *Language taught as a living means of communication.* Language is an instrument and its first aim is to be of use. Without language there can be no true communication between human beings: language is essentially an unceasing dialogue—a dialogue with other people and also with objects. It expresses a manner of being, of thinking, of feeling, of seeing people and things.

Language is not restricted to the rhythm of exchanged phrases: it develops through situations and it is inseparable from the movement of these situations. Any fact can, as soon as it is recognized, be expressed and interpreted through language: there is a close and solid association between situation and language. This is why the language should be taught from the outset as a means of expression and communication depending on all the resources of our being and with all the attitudes, gestures, mimicries, intonations and rhythms of spoken dialogue. The student must to some extent forget the role he has played since childhood with partners of his own nationality and tongue, and enter into the manner of being and of speaking of the French themselves.

In order to achieve this goal it is essential for the student to see and to come into close contact with real French characters speaking in French: these must be amusing and appealing, so that by entering their world the student identifies himself with them and adopts their language as he adopts the characters themselves.

These situations, presented by means of pictures, will constitute the first step: this is the beginning of communication, the recognition of a different reality, which must be understood and assimilated before partial identification with it takes place. Language will then become an integral part of this situation and will express it in a sound system different from that to which the student is accustomed, but which he will find easy to acquire because he is familiar with the situation itself. Once the student has mastered both the situation and the language which expresses it, communication becomes possible.

(3) *The use of audio-visual teaching techniques*. Once the principles of the method have been laid down it is obvious that recourse to pictures and sound reproduction becomes essential.

The picture is unique in that it makes possible the presentation and comprehension of numerous situations. For the time being filmstrips are considered preferable to film itself for practical reasons (low cost, easy use and stylization) and also for theoretical reasons: since the picture must always precede the relevant phrase by a few seconds and disappear only after this phrase has been spoken, the students' attention must be concentrated to the maximum so that situation and language are linked. Indeed, it would seem that the rhythm of this association and memorization is difficult to reconcile with the rhythm of the film, which is in continual movement.

The picture on the filmstrip can be projected for as long as the instructor judges useful: it is possible to wind the filmstrip back and forth and to show consecutively two images at opposite ends of the strip.

Perfect association between image and sound can be achieved only through the use of the tape-recorder, thereby also safeguarding the unity of the acoustic image of the language. Records present the same difficulty as film, for they work only in one direction: it is practically impossible to go back to a certain point in order to commence on a particular word.

The role of sound-recording is of great importance, for sounds, intonation and rhythm are registered as a whole by the listener. By recording groups of phonetics which each form a unity in sense and rhythm, and by integrating them into the range of intonations of the language to be learned, a powerful impression is made upon the brain, which is extremely sensitive to these rhythmic and melodic stimuli. The effect of these stimuli is strengthened by the synchronic association of recognition and memorization through sight and sound; this association recreates under experimental conditions the natural conditions for the acquisition of proficiency in a language.

Practical Use of the Method

Each of the thirty-two lessons in the course consists of a conversation between two or three people, with occasional interruptions from a commentator. This conversation deals with a centre of interest in everyday life. There is no question of dealing with every aspect of this centre of interest by naming or describing series of objects and actions but to demonstrate to the students the expressions which French people would have occasion to use in such situations.

These situations are presented on filmstrips, where the cartoons have been simplified so as to permit maximum concentration on a particular gesture or action or on the character who is speaking; the dialogues, closely linked to the cartoons, are recorded on tape. Each picture has a corresponding semantic group which expresses it in sound. The student must first of all hear the sound structure of this group and at the same time realize its meaning. During the course of the lesson he will repeat it and then learn to use it as a reflex action.

Each lesson has three parts: in the first part (*Sketch*), the stress is put on vocabulary, in the second part (*Mécanismes*) on grammar, and in the third part (*Phonétique*) on phonetics.

(1) *The sketch*. This is the part which presents the centre of interest; it is intended to teach constructions and vocabulary related to each of the themes treated.

The filmstrip should be placed in the projector ready for use before the students arrive. The first picture is shown immediately and fixes the centre of interest to be treated; the instructor presents this centre of interest by referring to the picture. The tape-recorder is switched on and the tape started so that the first semantic group of the lesson is heard immediately. The film-strip is presented in its entirety and synchronized with the tape-recording. The length of the silence after each group in the text has been carefully calculated so as to allow the student time to take in the situation shown on the picture, hear the sound group which refers to it, and, at a later stage of the lesson, which will be described, to repeat it. The passing from one picture to the next must be clear and rapid, and the picture must always appear at least one second before the appropriate sound group.

The lesson is then shown in the same way a second time, as the students themselves feel the need for this. Later on, however, by the time Lesson 20 has been reached, and the students' eyes have been trained to take in a situation at once and their hearing exercised, a single presentation will be sufficient.

From Lessons 4 and 5 onwards the instructor asks the pupils to repeat from memory what they have heard; naturally there is no question of getting a perfect or complete repetition. The exercise must be carried out rapidly and the instructor should not correct mistakes, merely acknowledging the students' efforts by *Yes* or *No*. He should not, however, disregard any corrections proposed by the students themselves. The instructor can therefore note the phrases which have been correctly heard by the majority of students and which will therefore not need to be dealt with at great length later on, as well as those which have been incorrectly heard, and judge from the replies those phrases which have not been heard at all.

Initially, it is essential to make sure that the students hear all the semantic groups in the text, and that they understand them. The filmstrip is shown again, one picture at a time, and the tape-recorder stopped after each group which has not been heard and understood by the whole class. Thanks to the rapid rewind mechanism on the tape-recorder, the same group can be played over several times consecutively. The instructor should not be

C

too eager to substitute his own voice for that of the loudspeaker; it is only when all else seems to have failed that he should do so, and even then he must imitate the voice recorded on the tape without giving too much importance to the part of the passage in a particular semantic group which has not been understood by saying it out of context or by emphasizing it. For example, in Lesson 9: *Paul, viens voir à la fenêtre*. If the student has heard *Viens voir la fenêtre* the instructor must take great care not to detach the 'à'. The point is not that the student has not heard the sound 'à' (which he hears in la, ma, madame, etc.), but that he has not taken in the rhythm of the group as a whole, which must never be destroyed, since comprehension should always be preceded by perfect hearing.

In order to explain, the instructor first of all uses the picture: with an electric pointer-torch or ordinary pointer, he draws the students' attention to the parts of the cartoon which will help comprehension of the group, commencing with those which should already be familiar to the students. From the elements which are already known he continues by asking question after question about those which are not understood, thereby bringing out their sense and phonetic form by situating them in the sound and semantic structure of the group.

Once the semantic groups have been perfectly heard and understood, the students should repeat them by imitating as closely as possible the recorded phonetic groups while the pictures are being shown. Both from the point of view of correct pronunciation, and from that of rhythm and intonation, the success of the method depends on perfect imitation of these groups.

During the first lessons of the course this repetition exercise is done only in the classroom, and it is essential that each student should repeat individually every group in the lesson. The recorded group is played on the tape-recorder, and the students asked to repeat it one by one; during the repetition of a particular group by all the students the recording should be replayed several times. The instructor must be very strict with this exercise, although, of course, it is unlikely that perfect imitation will be obtained during the first few lessons; when he thinks that a particular student will not make any more progress at that moment he should pass on to the next.

When a language laboratory is available for individual work the repetition exercise should take place there. However, this does not necessarily mean that the student will immediately be able to compare his own recording with that on the tape. Long and strict training is necessary before the student is able to correct himself. The instructor listens to the student's recording, and if there is a mistake he stops the tape and plays the master recording over until the student repeats it correctly; then he makes the student compare what he has just said with his first attempt at repetition, and goes on to make him record correctly. This work in the laboratory does not eliminate the necessity for repetition in class, but it does give more rapid results.

How to use the contents of the lesson. At this stage, expressions not contained within the vocabulary of the particular lesson should not be taught unless they are given accidentally; here there is no need to bring in new vocabulary, even if it is closely related to the centre of interest in question, but use should be made of vocabulary in the lesson and in preceding lessons.

Once the expressions are fixed in the student's memory, he should be asked to repeat them spontaneously, as a reflex, when he is shown the situation to which they apply. The first exercise consists of showing the filmstrip through without using the tape-recorder, and asking the student to reproduce the dialogue for each picture. As he makes progress it will be noticed that the student is no longer content with repeating only the text in question but frequently substitutes other useful expressions using forms and structures which he has already studied.

How the filmstrip should be used. Certain pictures are merely transitional, for the course has been designed so that each sound group in the text has a corresponding image. There is no need to devote much time to these transitional phrases, which generally show a character in the foreground pronouncing a word or short expression with an expressive gesture, such as *Oui, Non, Bien sûr* and so on.

The other pictures represent scenes with characters in a particular attitude, doing certain actions or making certain gestures: 'balloons' similar to those in comic-strips indicate what the characters are discussing, and what has been, or will be, done. The students should be trained to describe rapidly each picture by using the structures given in the lessons.

How the lesson should be used without the filmstrip. By asking questions about the 'story' told in the lesson, the instructor encourages the students to converse both with him and with each other; they should also be trained to ask each other questions, which the instructor may correct, if he considers it to be necessary.

During this exercise the centre of interest of the lesson is developed, without the addition of much extra vocabulary, and the questions are made to apply to the student's own life and background.

Series of questions are recorded on tape for use in the language laboratory; a space is left on the tape after each question so that the student can record his reply, and then an example of an appropriate reply is given on the tape. From Lesson 25 onwards these exercises may be done in writing.

(2) *Mécanismes* (*grammatical structures*). Although the lesson itself includes the study of a centre of interest designed to teach a limited vocabulary and related structures, the accompanying *mécanismes* are designed to study one or several grammar points out of the whole which makes up the first part of Fundamental French (*le français fondamental, 1er degré*).

The instructor should see that the student makes an effort to understand the sense of the complete structure and then to use it in as many different examples as possible, until he acquires the reflex mechanism necessary for spontaneous use of the structure under consideration.

The progression of the method over thirty-two lessons presented various problems of priorities. It was essential to begin with the ideas without which communication is impossible; these essential notions (verbs *être* (to be) and *avoir* (to have), use of indefinite and definite articles and possessive adjectives) provide the basis of Lessons 1 to 6. The student must first of all study, and learn to use as a reflex, the elements which will enable him to communicate with other people (*je suis—vous êtes—qui est-ce?*—*c'est* ...) and to take his place vis-à-vis other people and also objects (*qu'est-ce que c'est ?—c'est un* ...—*c'est une* ...—*ce sont des* ...—*c'est mon* ... *ma* ..., etc.—*qu'est-ce qu'il y a sur* ... *sous* ... *dans* ... etc.)

The mechanisms in the first six lessons are composed of a series of short dialogues, in each of which the grammatical structure to be studied is given by means of a situation presented through an image. These dialogues or situations described by a commentator are not related to each other except through the grammatical structures which they present.

Once these fundamental elements have been assimilated, the progression of the course is designed mainly to give:

(a) practice in the use of the most commonly used verbs (*aller*, *faire*, *venir*, reflexive verbs in affirmative, negative and interrogative phrases in the tenses most often used in conversation: present, future, imperative, perfect and recent past tenses);

(b) practice in the spontaneous use of personal pronouns (especially complementary pronouns associated in complex groups such as: *Il me l'a dit; je ne lui donne pas; apporte m'en un*, etc.)

From Lesson 7 onwards, the *mécanismes* are more concerned with one particular difficulty of the French language.

(3) *Phonétique (Practical phonetics)*. In this audio-visual course the study of the sound-system forms an integral part of the basic principles of the method, which, since its point of departure is the spoken language, deals consistently with the acoustic aspects of the

language. It is a structural method where grammatical elements are not taken into account, and phonetic exercises are found in all three parts of each lesson; indeed, intonation and rhythm are of great importance for the assimilation of the spoken text.

The foreign student learns most French sounds as such through the acoustic unity of the phrase as produced through the intonation. Thus, through the structures, sounds as well as words will gradually be assimilated. This is why the instructor must insist on the most faithful reproduction of the intonation in all parts of the lesson; this reproduction is a physiological stimulus which enables the groups of phrases to be retained in the foreigner's brain.

At the beginning of the course the instructor must take into consideration the fact that students do not hear certain French sounds correctly, for everyone hears sounds only in relation to those of his mother-tongue. This is why the student learning a foreign language for the first time always defends in his subconscious the means of expression which his mother-tongue has given him: he opposes the characteristics of his mother-tongue to those of the foreign language as a kind of self-defence.

It can therefore be said that anyone learning a foreign language acts as though he were hard of hearing. But as both ear and brain function structurally, this method is designed to present sounds through structures—intonation and rhythm—thereby permitting the student to acquire the correct pronunciation not only of French rhythm and intonation, but also of French sounds as such.

The third part of each lesson gives particular attention to phonetics so that the instructor can methodically follow a rational progression and give special attention in each lesson to certain sounds. As this part of the lesson is also given in the form of a dialogue, the structural form of the method is safeguarded. It should be noted that correct reproduction of intonation and rhythm is much more important than correct pronunciation of one sound; the instructor should never, therefore, sacrifice rhythm and intonation to the correct pronunciation of particular French sounds.

III. Written Language in the Audio-visual Method

It must be clearly stated why, initially, a completely oral method was adopted. The written language is not the language itself but merely a means of representing it through a purely conventional graphic system. French spelling, although basically phonetic, abounds in anomalies which are rooted in its etymological, historical and grammatical character. In fact, if the student is confronted at the very beginning with a text it does not help him, but, on the contrary, provides a mass of difficulties which he is incapable, at this stage, of surmounting; moreover, it is most undesirable to give the student, at the beginning of his studies, the idea that the writing of French is confused and difficult to learn.

The whole audio-visual method is based on the study of the language structures through intonation and rhythm. The mere sight of letters familiar to us is sufficient to produce the automatic reaction of articulation, and as written French transcribes neither rhythm nor intonation, and contains a large number of anomalies (double consonants) and unpronounced letters (plural noun- and adjective-endings, verb-endings, mute *e*, etc.), all these tend to encourage the student to make mistakes.

The student who learns through written language (or even through phonetic notation) at once associates this form with the sense and claims that he cannot understand what he has not seen written: he makes little effort to hear what is said in French, consequently hearing less, and eventually can no longer hear at all unless he has the written text to consult. He can express himself only by thinking first of the written form and then speaking. Conversation becomes impossible unless the student rapidly gets into the habit of passing straight from sound to sense in order to understand, and from sense to sound in order to express himself.

Moreover, a written text encourages excessive analysis, and this means that the essential aim of global recognition of the sense of the semantic group is neglected; the student has to worry about spelling and grammatical problems, and the reader, wishing to understand every single work, refers automatically to the corresponding work in a language familiar to him: this leads inevitably to literal translation.

Teachers tend to adhere to the old tradition of relying only on the visual memory and almost always neglecting the auditive memory: this tradition is highly questionable. Experience proves that the child's auditive memory is extremely rich but loses its efficiency if it is not sufficiently exercised. The adult student's auditive memory must be revived and trained so that he may eventually come to feel entirely at ease when relying only on his hearing.

It is therefore essential that the method should, at the outset, be entirely phonetic, so that the texts of the lessons should not be shown to the students. The instructor's efforts should be concentrated on making the students hear, distinguish and reproduce sound groups; on getting them to recognize the complete sense of semantic groups, and on teaching the *mécanismes* (language structure and grammatical mechanisms) and getting students to use them spontaneously.

IV. The Use of Cinema in the Teaching of French

In collaboration with the *Centre Audio-Visuel* at Saint-Cloud, the *Centre de Recherches et d'Études pour la Diffusion du Français* has in the past two years produced a number of films intended for students learning French. This series of films is experimental, and by using various types of film, their respective value in language teaching, as well as the most efficient techniques, have been tested.

(1) *Films to Help in the Revision of Points Already Learnt*

During the lessons the students study various different centres of interest (*la circulation, le jardin public, la campagne, un jour de travail, les vacances*, etc.). They are familiar with the vocabulary and common structures relating to these themes. The films deal with the same themes and are presented after the lessons. The students are then encouraged to talk about what they have seen on the screen, and are thus given the opportunity of putting what they have learnt to an immediate practical use.

These films have been made in two different ways:

(a) without commentary: the student himself has to provide the commentary in this case, and under the influence of the animated film he makes the necessary effort of his own accord. The film must therefore produce a reaction from the student by showing actions and incidents which he can easily recall and describe after the film has been shown.

(b) films with commentary: the student hears expressions familiar to him, but in a new context and applied to the situations shown in the film. After the showing of the film it has been noticed that the student uses these expressions again spontaneously and correctly, which leads one to suppose that films with commentary can, if carefully adapted to suit the student's level, be an excellent method of fixing in his mind the structures and vocabulary learnt in class.

However, in this type of film the commentary must be carefully chosen. At what level should it be situated? Will it be of any use with students who have not learnt French by the audio-visual method? All the possibilities must be exploited, but it has been proved that the showing of a film with commentary enables the instructor to widen the range of discussion with his students.

(2) *Films Designed to Teach New Points*

Two texts from the audio-visual lessons were selected and two films were made based on these texts, using the same dialogue as in the lessons. The first film presents a fresh centre of interest,

Le téléphone. The second, entitled *Un homme tranquille*, is a film on the use of the perfect tense conjugated with *avoir*.

The student probably learns the lesson better from filmstrips with stylized pictures and slow presentation, but film itself has a much wider range of use.

A film has also been made on the use of the perfect and imperfect tenses; it is designed to initiate the student into the use of these past tenses which are so difficult to employ correctly.

Use of the Film

These films are not intended solely for students who have learnt French by the audio-visual method, and they can be used to complement any other method because they illustrate facts about the language and show scenes from French life.

It has been proved that slides can be of great assistance when used to accompany a film. After the showing of the film the student finds it easy to talk about the story and the incidents or actions which he particularly noticed; however, many of the scenes in the film will have escaped his attention or cannot be clearly recollected, and the slides, when shown at this point, will help the student to give a full description of a particular situation. Moreover, slides showing places or buildings of interest can be used as documentation for preparatory classes in French culture. There are also a number of literary texts closely linked in content to the slides and films.

When integrated in this way with other teaching techniques film can be extremely useful in the early stages of learning a language, for knowledge of the language alone is incomplete and useless unless the student is familiar with the country and people for whom it is the mother-tongue.

4. Teaching Languages by Radio

Jean Rowntree

WHEN the first post-war language teaching programmes for adults were broadcast by the BBC in 1954 they went out to a hypothetical public on the basis of what turned out to be some not very good guesses. They consisted of *Brush Up Your French* programmes for adult listeners who were assumed to have learnt French at school, to have forgotten most of what they had learned and who now—provided no real effort was involved—wanted to revive it so as to make better use of their French holidays. Ten minutes was thought to be the limit of their attention, even to programmes planned to be entertaining: no homework was expected or provided.

This tentative beginning could hardly have been avoided. In 1954 there was no Third Network to offer a service for serious minorities: French lessons were intruders into the Home Service, a programme for general listening, and had to earn their place as entertainment. Nor could the BBC be blamed for failing to realize its potentialities for serious language teaching. In the early fifties the post-war travel boom was not at its peak, and though foreign travel was increasing, it had not yet had a significant effect on the learning of languages. The existence of a growing public of adult listeners prepared to study not only French and German but Italian, Spanish and Russian from the beginning only became evident some time later.

For the next four years language programmes were gradually extended, in no case without misgivings, none of which turned out in the event to have been justified. French programmes were continued on roughly the original pattern; a course in Italian was followed by a course in German.

Very little was known about the public for these programmes, and a good many guesses proved to be wrong. The adult listener did not like the use of dramatization: he did not need to be cajoled into taking a language seriously; he disapproved, even, of the use of documentary material when its technical quality was not up to standard. If you really want to learn Italian the bells of Perugia are no substitute for an audible voice.

As time went on each course produced its own evidence, and a picture began to take shape. Correspondence and Audience Research reports made it clear that the lessons were getting near their target, and by 1957, when all language programmes were transferred from the Home Service to the Third Network without reducing the number of listeners, it was evident that they were meeting the needs and interests of a growing number of people.

In 1959 the first beginners series was broadcast, and a small revolution occurred which it took several years to understand. The audience grew to almost three times its previous size: where a good 'Brush Up' booklet might sell from 20 to 40,000 copies at most, *Russian for Beginners* sold about 60,000, most of them in the early weeks of the series. This increase was at first attributed to the novelty of the language and the shortage of other means of learning it. But when *Italian for Beginners* was broadcast in 1960 and *German for Beginners* in 1962, their sales were about the same: some other explanation had to be found.

At the same time it was evident that the character of the audience was beginning to change. Correspondence now included letters from listeners who were not, apparently, used to expressing themselves easily in their own language: there was some perplexity over grammatical terms, and one writer said that she now knew what the nominative and accusative were in Russian, but what were they in English? Producers began to be doubtful what, if any, basic grammar they could expect their public to possess.

It is easy today to see what had happened. Beginners series were attracting large numbers of listeners who had already learned one language and wanted to start another: they were also drawing on the interest of a small but growing number of people who had missed the chance of grammar school education. Some of these—a fair proportion, I would judge—were unlikely at this stage to have joined an evening class, with the act of commitment that this involves, and seem to have been attracted to radio as a means of learning because, at no greater cost than the price of a 5s. handbook, it offered many of the advantages of direct instruction without the accompanying disadvantage of making one's mistakes in public.

From the educationist's point of view this second group is by far the most significant. It is true that it is not a large one: only some 12% of the listeners to the first Russian beginners series had left school at fifteen or earlier. But Russian is a special case: those who learn it are less likely to be influenced by tourist motives than those who are attracted to courses in German or Italian. Indeed, the majority of people who bought the booklet said that they did so because Russian was 'a language one ought to know'. For other European languages one might expect a higher proportion of students outside the grammar school tradition, and it may well be for this reason that Russian has so far shown less capacity for growth once the initial interest has been tapped: when the first Russian beginners series was repeated the sales of the booklet were only one-sixth of the original figure, whereas an Italian beginners series sold one-third of the original number of booklets for its repeat series. At the other end of the scale French may also be a special case, and a French beginners series—such as the one in 1964—may well attract a large proportion of listeners who have had no previous opportunity of learning a language. But small or large—and it seems to be increasing—this new audience is clearly an important one for radio; even, perhaps, for modern school education: what is more doubtful is the extent to which it can be passed on from the radio apprenticeship to adult education proper. I shall return to this question later.

Just how serious is the radio language public? There can be no doubt that the great majority of listeners start out prepared to work hard with the object of acquiring the mastery of a language. From 1955 onwards there has been a steady demand for longer and more serious programmes, more homework, more repeats and more pure instruction. There is, of course, a certain fall-off in listening to any forty-week series which makes demands not only on the student's concentration but on his free time: even in the most popular programme some decline is to be expected. In 1962, for instance, when a German beginners course was planned in two halves, with a summer break in the middle, a separate booklet was prepared for each half of the course, and the sales for the second booklet were just over half the sales of the first one: in *Russian for Beginners*, initially broadcast from 1959 to 1960, the decline was a good deal sharper. Taking as a sample some 1000 people who bought the booklet in the early months of the course, Audience Research carried out a full inquiry into their persistence in listening and their reasons for giving it up: the proportion that persisted was 25%. Of those who gave up the majority had found the time inconvenient, had missed one lesson and were unable to catch up, or had found that the course demanded more time than they were able to spare. Although this last reason may be to some extent a form of rationalization, there is no doubt that a course of this sort does demand a great deal more of the listener than the twenty or forty minutes a week he spends at the radio, and that once he begins to cut down his homework it is only a matter of time before he gives up the broadcasts as well.

So far as methods are concerned it has to be recognized that although radio can do a few things superlatively well there are only a limited number of things that it can do at all. Music, noise, silence and the human voice are its only building materials, and language lessons are usually restricted to the last two. It is true that some early programmes made use of music, mainly for its entertainment value, and the first Russian beginners course introduced the sound of the telephone or musical instrument as an integral part of the programme in order to make up for listeners' absence of vocabulary. Music has now been given up in response to the demand for more austere treatment, and programmes which have to supplement the student's lack of vocabulary would now more properly be placed in television.

The main virtue of radio in this context is the opportunity it provides for the listener to hear the sounds and rhythm of a different language. In Russian, for instance, the whole pattern is unfamiliar: we have no memory framework in which to place the sounds we hear. It is only after we have gone on listening for a certain time that a memory structure can be built up, and this is true whether we understand the meaning of the words or not. Once this structure is established, the association of ideas may follow very quickly: several of the students who started Russian in a series for beginners in 1959, and went on in 1961 to a much more difficult course, commented on the break-through that takes place when the ear has been accustomed for some time to memorizing unfamiliar noises and they suddenly begin to make sense. Anyone with a good ear can develop an aural memory: it is only a question of use and custom. If you hear a tuning-fork week after week it will not be surprising if you develop absolute pitch; and a child will very soon learn from the inflection of his parent's voice whether it is safe to disobey him or not. When radio begins to experiment with Chinese this factor will be crucial, because the listener's ability to learn a tonal language depends, in the first place, on an accurate aural memory.

The association of sound and meaning is, of course, dependent to a great extent on the pace of teaching, and I doubt if it is always recognized that the wrong pace, even in English, may give its hearers the impression that a spoken text is incomprehensible, when it would be well within their grasp if they saw it in print. Many years ago a sample programme on consumer economics was played experimentally to a group of women who were unable to take in any part of it when it ran the fifteen minutes proposed, though they found it perfectly simple at twenty-six minutes. Before the first beginners Russian series a programme planned to run for fifteen minutes was played to a sample audience, who agreed that the same amount of material would be suitable for a twenty-minute programme. All of us have our own pace of comprehension, and radio teaching must find a compromise which satisfies as many of its students as possible, though with a public ranging from modern school leavers to university professors this is by no means an easy thing to do.

The pace of teaching is, of course, a separate problem from the pace at which a foreign language is actually spoken. For this there must be different speeds, which will differ from series to series and from programme to programme. It is important that as early as possible students should have the opportunity of listening to a language at the pace at which they would hear it spoken in its own country, even if this means that it must then be repeated, if necessary several times over.

Comprehension depends also on the use of silence; and the right placing of silence, important in any sound broadcast, is essential in a language programme, not only so that the listener can absorb what he has heard but also because of the occasions where he is asked to repeat a word or phrase and must be given time to use his lips and tongue in what may well be an unfamiliar way.

These points concern radio language teaching in general. There are others that apply particularly to lessons for adults, which, unlike school programmes, go out for the most part to individuals listening at home. From them there is no 'live' teacher to supply a context: he has to be built in; and this means that the lessons cannot be given entirely in the language itself: even if the majority of the teaching framework is transferred to a printed booklet, *some* English there must be, if only a page reference. The absence of a 'live' teacher, together with the limitation of the sound medium, and the expectations of the adult student, combine to present the radio language producer with some formidable problems, and it is not easy in these circumstances to make much use of the modern audio-visual methods of teaching. For one thing, the adult listener is impatient of anything that seems to slow him down, and the admirable methods used, for instance, by the Language Laboratory at

Ealing require 250 hours of instruction alone. In a forty-lesson radio beginners course the student who listens to both hearings of the lessons will be committed to less than twenty-seven hours of instruction, and that is probably the most it will ever be realistic to expect broadcasting to provide.

This comparison does, I think, illustrate one of the toughest problems of radio language teaching, and it brings me to a point I have touched on already—the fact that results can be achieved from broadcast lessons only if the listener is prepared to put in a good deal more time than he spends simply in listening. The difficulty is that the majority of adult listeners have to do their preparation at the end of a working day, and this sets a definite limit to the amount of work that can be expected of them: in a recent Russian course, for example, many people found that they could only keep up with the lessons at all if they could spend six evenings on preparation, and this, with the best will in the world, they were quite unable to do.

It would be easy to say that, given X hours as the maximum time for preparation, forty beginners lessons will only be able to reach objective Y. The difficulty is that in many cases the adult listener *expects* to get to objective Z, and would not have attempted the course at all unless he had thought it possible. To this dilemma no answer has yet been found—except to broadcast a course at a pace that leaves no time for consolidation, in the hope that the student will be able to fill in the gaps when it comes to an end. No one would consider this an ideal solution. For one thing it dictates a form of teaching considered by many professional linguists to be out of date—though this, it should be said, is not a complaint that is often made by the listener. Probably the right method will only be found by trial and error: ready-made solutions are certainly not the answer; and since most audio-visual methods draw on four elements—film, tape, print and a 'live' teacher, of which sound programmes for adults possess only two, some adaptation will be essential if they are to be used in a radio context.

It is probably in the relation between the spoken and the

written word that new methods will have to be found, and this will not be difficult, because all language courses, except some of the readings for advanced students, have their own booklet. These vary in size according to the level of difficulty: for beginners they offer something like a self-contained handbook. At the same time it is assumed that the serious student will possess his own dictionary and probably his own primer: only one series has even attempted to provide a full-scale grammar. The main purpose of these booklets is to allow him to prepare for the lesson in advance and to go over it in retrospect: this is an extension of time rather than a transfer of the learning process from ear to eye, and no course can offer the student anything durable unless it provides him with these extra hours.

In its search for the ideal method of teaching radio must not lose sight of the special character of its public. It is not in question that its programmes should be useful and real. But these are relative terms, and the radio audience is a very mixed one: some people listen for vocational reasons; some because they are interested in literature and impatient of translations; some, perhaps the greater proportion, because, for business or tourist reasons, they want to visit a foreign country. But even if broadcasting were to concentrate mainly on this last group, should it not aim at something more than a guide-book situation, in which tourists are prepared—and no more—to hold their own against the possibly unhelpful foreigner? Travel today does not consist of the Grand Tour, nor does it consist only of *Le Camping*. When we go abroad we want to do more than ask the way to the post office or the price of a hotel bed: we want, if possible, to talk to people on equal terms—about politics and ideas, about what we do in our free time, how we bring up our children, and what we read and think and eat. For this we need *literature*—(in which I would include articles, plays, the sound-track of film, current satire and cookery books) as well as conversation—we need the bricks as well as the tools of a language. The BBC is sometimes urged to be less 'literary' in its approach and, so far as its elementary programmes are concerned, this advice is probably sound. In its advanced programmes the problems are different, and the choice of content is surely as important as the choice of method.

Today, in 1965, broadcast language lessons are at a cross-roads. The first BBC television course for adults is now being broadcast: sound courses, firmly established as an essential service, are being reviewed to see how far they can be adapted to new methods: the possibility of an experimental service in minority languages (Chinese and Arabic, for example) is being explored; and a project is being considered by which the tapes of language courses are loaned, for a small fee, to educational organizations. In a year's time it will be possible to speak a good deal more confidently about new possibilities in broadcast language teaching. Today I can only suggest some of the ways in which it seems likely that they may be affected by previous experience.

In the first place, what is the demarcation line between courses in sound and TV? Do they serve a different public, or simply perform a different function? TV courses certainly have a larger public and one which may be less inclined to spend time on preparation than the audience for the sound programmes. They may therefore attract a mass public to the *idea* of learning a language, and pass on a proportion of their viewers either to class instruction or to the more advanced courses in sound radio. On the other hand there is no doubt that the public for sound programmes is a highly selective one which follows its courses on any programme service and (though not without protest) at almost any time of day. Such listeners, if they possess a TV set, will probably be *included* in the TV public. What, then, are the respective roles of sound and TV?

The answer to this question is not so simple as it seems. Both media are adapted to an oral approach which presents the language in a living context and encourages the student to use it as well as learn it. Television is indeed particularly well suited to this. But the amount of repetition involved in the modern forms of language teaching would be extravagant of air time in an expensive medium and it might prove tedious to the larger television public: the same is true of grammatical explanation, which, in its early stages, might otherwise be more effective in television than in sound.

There is a further point. When those of us concerned in educational broadcasting begin to think out the proper spheres of the two media, we always come back to the same distinction. In science, for example, the early stages are obviously more appropriate to television than to sound. But once a subject is concerned with abstract relationships, sound is often the better medium: it offers the listener the two things he needs for the acceptance of a concept—words and silence—whereas TV is bound to show something on the screen, if only a speaker's face. At the point therefore, where grammar begins to deal with complexities that cannot be illustrated, it is no more appropriate to television than it is to sound—perhaps less so. Yet a high proportion of grammar and syntax is inappropriate even in a radio course: perhaps its only proper place is in the booklet that accompanies it.

Until we have more experience it is obviously easier to ask questions about television language teaching than it is to find the answers. What is clear is that while television offers only one language course a year, it is likely to stimulate an interest it cannot satisfy, and it may be that, in future, radio will be less concerned with beginners, at any rate in the language covered by television, and will concentrate on offering a wide variety of language at a rather different level.

A word about minority languages. Sound radio is interested in offering a service for the serious minority, and intensity of listening, together with the value of the service provided, will certainly be offset against the reduction of the audience. But there is a limit to the shrinkage that can be accepted, even by public service broadcasting, and minority language courses are unlikely to be broadcast unless their public can be shown to be capable of some expansion. Chinese is a case in point. The demand for classes is increasing very fast. It is the only UN language not so far included in the sound radio schedule. It is a tonal language, in which the ear plays a crucial part, and there are not enough teachers or good Chinese voices to meet the demand for lessons. (Most of the voices to be heard in Chinese restaurants are Cantonese: the BBC course would be broadcast in the national language.) Moreover, sound radio would be well qualified to offer a pronunciation course, in which the problem of Chinese characters is indefinitely postponed. An experimental programme is to be made on these lines and tried out on close circuit to sample listeners. If it succeeds it will be followed by a course of experimental broadcasts.

Finally, there is the scheme for the loan of tapes to educational organizations. I have left this to the end because it raises a point that is central to the whole question of broadcast language lessons—indeed to educational broadcasting as a whole. Put at its simplest the question is whether broadcasting should be considered as an ancillary to formal adult education or as an educational process in its own right. There is a good deal to be said on both sides, but so far as languages are concerned one factor is not on the side of the ancillary process, and that is numbers. All the evidence suggests that by far the greater proportion of adult students following the BBC language courses consists of individuals listening at home—people who for geographical or personal reasons are outside the reach of class teaching. The greater part of our correspondence comes not from students but from retired people, sick people, women tied to the house, the 'enclosed religious', business men planning a special project, young people planning a holiday. Only a small proportion of these are likely to graduate to class work, but there can be no doubt that in catering for their interests, broadcasting is doing an important service. This is not to say that some part of the language output should not be geared to class purposes, or that some programmes—readings for advanced students, for example—could not, in fact, serve both purposes. It may also be possible to process some of the conversation lessons for sale commercially, transferring the English instruction contained in them to a printed leaflet.

It is in this context that the new plan for hiring the tapes of language lessons has to be considered. So far this has gone no further than the launching of a pilot scheme; and though, in the end, it could grow into something big, a number of questions must be answered first—for example, would educational organizations prefer to make their own recordings of BBC series? (this is a breach of copyright, but there is no doubt that it is being done) or would they rather pay for the convenience of not being tied to a specific time, for a tape of guaranteed quality, and for having what, as the scheme developed, would become in the end a wide choice of courses in different languages and at different levels? Would class teachers in all but the most difficult languages prefer (if they used them at all) to recommend BBC courses to their students as a form of required reading and not to absorb them into the main stream of teaching? Would some educational organizations—Women's Institutes and Townswomen's Guilds, for example—consider hiring a beginners programme, and organizing teacherless classes on their own premises? And could this scheme be extended to industry? The evidence suggests that this may be the most promising development of all. Answers to these questions are urgently needed, because they will determine the extent to which radio programmes should be self-contained. Until they are available it would, I think, be unwise to give up too much of a limited schedule to programmes that cannot stand on their own feet.

In all this uncertainty there is one point on which those of us who have watched the development of radio language programmes have no doubts. Language teaching today has a social and national importance it never had before. The first duty of broadcasting is to build on a growing interest in languages and to do everything it can to extend it. It is the non-professional linguist who will talk business to the German and the Italian: it is the non-professional linguist who is concerned with the underdeveloped countries. Radio can do something for the student—it is in any case dependent on the skills and authority of the professional linguist—but it should, I think, resist the demand—a demand that is already becoming evident—to adapt itself exclusively to the needs of class teaching. Broadcasting is a profession as well as a form of communication, and it has its own skills and its own techniques. What has to be done in the next few years is to find a way to marry the best broadcasting techniques with the best in language teaching so that it can provide a social and not simply an academic service, and act as a stimulus as well as a buttress to learning.

Forty years of broadcasting has made good music generally accessible and disposed of the myth that we are not a musical nation. May not ten years of language teaching do the same for the myth that we have no gift for languages ?

APPENDIX

The Expansion of BBC Sound Radio Language Teaching Series 1954–64

SERIES	LEVEL	NUMBER OF PRO-GRAMMES IN SERIES	LENGTH OF PRO-GRAMME (min.)	SERVICE
1954–5				
FRENCH				
En Voyage Series 1	Intermediate	8	10	Home
En Voyage Series 2	Intermediate	10	10	Home
1955–6				
FRENCH				
Entente Cordiale	Intermediate	13	15	Home
ITALIAN				
Assignment in Italy	Intermediate	13	15	Home
GERMAN				
Gute Reise!	Intermediate	13	15	Home
1956–7				
FRENCH				
En Famille	Intermediate	20	15	Home
GERMAN				
Wiedersehen in Deutschland	Intermediate	20	15	Home

SERIES	LEVEL	NUMBER OF PROGRAMMES IN SERIES	LENGTH OF PROGRAMME (min.)	SERVICE
1957–8				
FRENCH				
The French on the French Series 1	Advanced	11	15	Net. 3
Le Mot Juste	Intermediate	15	15	Net. 3
The French on the French Series 2	Advanced	14	15	Net. 3
GERMAN				
Starting German	Simple	21	15	Net. 3
Three Men in a Boat	Advanced	8	15	Net. 3
SPANISH				
Starting Spanish	Simple	20	15	Net. 3
1958–9				
FRENCH				
The French on the French Series 3	Advanced	11	20	Net. 3
Brains Trust (Talking German)	Advanced	6	15	Net. 3
Talking German (Brush-up)	Intermediate	6	20	Net. 3
ITALIAN				
Italian Journey	Intermediate	26	15	Net. 3
1959–60				
FRENCH				
Anthologie	Advanced	12	20	Net. 3
The French on the French Series 4	Advanced	4	20	Net. 3
GERMAN				
Improve Your German Series 1	Intermediate	22	20	Net. 3
RUSSIAN				
Russian for Beginners	Beginners (1st true beginners series)	41	20	Net. 3
Russian by Interview	Advanced	7	20	Net. 3

SERIES	LEVEL	NUMBER OF PRO-GRAMMES IN SERIES	LENGTH OF PRO-GRAMME (min)	SERVICE
1960–1				
GERMAN				
Improve Your German Series 2	Intermediate	22	20	Net. 3
ITALIAN				
Italian for Beginners	Beginners	40	20	Net. 3
RUSSIAN				
Keep Up Your Russian	Intermediate	20	20	Net. 3
1961–2				
FRENCH				
Keep Up Your French	Intermediate	20	20	Net. 3
GERMAN				
Albumblätter (schools rept.)	Advanced	18	20	Net. 3
German for Beginners Part 1	Beginners	20	20	Net. 3
ITALIAN				
Keep Up Your Italian	Intermediate	20	20	Net.
Italian Readings	Advanced	9	20	Net.
RUSSIAN				
Russian Readings	Advanced	20	20	Net. 3
1962–3				
FRENCH				
French Readings	Advanced	12	20	Net. 3
GERMAN				
German for Beginners Part 2	Beginners	21	20	Net. 3
ITALIAN				
Use Your Italian	Intermediate	20	20	Net. 3
RUSSIAN				
Starting Russian	Beginners	41	20	Net. 3
Use Your Russian	Advanced	12	20	Net. 3

SERIES	LEVEL	NUMBER OF PRO-GRAMMES IN SERIES	LENGTH OF PRO-GRAMME (min)	SERVICE
1963–4				
FRENCH				
Keep up your French	Intermediate	20	20	Net. 3
French Readings	Advanced	9	20	Net. 3
ITALIAN				
Use Your Italian	Intermediate	20	20	Net. 3
GERMAN				
German for Beginners	Beginners	41	20	Net. 3
SPANISH				
Spanish for Beginners	Beginners	40	20	Net. 3
RUSSIAN				
Use Your Russian	Intermediate	12	20	Net. 3

Note: If this article had been written in 1964 the emphasis might have been rather different, and more could have been said about the comparative response to language courses in Television and Radio—e.g. that the multiplier for Television (less than half, judged by the sale of beginners' booklets in the same language) is not so large as might have been expected. The picture of Radio language teaching it contains is, however, still accurate.

5. The Liberal Approach in a Large Centre

H. A. JONES, MA and MICHAEL HAY, MA

THE teaching of modern languages has always occupied a dubious place in English adult education. The assumption seems to have been that proficiency in a foreign language was a skill like plumbing, and desirable only for commercial ends; so it has been lumped with the vocational range of subjects and entrusted to LEA institutions.

Perhaps because of this the teaching of foreign languages as a liberal activity has been almost unknown. Adult students have either had to join examination courses at 'O' or 'A' level (and have done so uncomplainingly, because this was the only kind of language teaching they had encountered at school); or they were catered for in 'conversation' classes in evening institutes, supposed to be for tourists, but often doing little real work and existing as social rather than educational units. Yet many adults do seek the serious study of foreign languages for other than vocational reasons, and the various agencies for adult education have been made increasingly aware of this demand in recent years.

The position has been confused by what has for long seemed to be the Ministry of Education view that the teaching of a language to adults is appropriate for provision by LEA's because they teach the skills and the practical subjects, and that the so-called responsible bodies (university extramural departments and the WEA) should teach only the literature, history and institutions of the country, preferably in English.

In this confused situation the London literary institutes have been fortunately placed. Founded to afford a wide range of non-vocational classes for adults in the liberal traditions of the

Responsible Bodies, they were able, being L E A institutions, to relate their studies of foreign literatures to a programme of language classes, and to set these in a context of general studies in literature, history, art, archaeology, drama, music, philosophy and so on, rather than in the context of practical and recreational classes of the general evening institute or the context of examination classes of the college of further education.

Most fortunate perhaps has been the City Literary Institute because, having premises of its own, it has been able to develop specialized classes in the daytime as well as the usual range of evening classes; and the size of its total programme has enabled it to offer sets of parallel classes in each language, so that students could be graded according to their abilities on entry to secure some homogeneity of standard.

In 1960 it became possible for the Institute to establish a department of modern languages with a full-time head, believed to have been the first such appointment in any non-vocational institution. The intention in setting up the department was that the various approaches to the teaching of modern languages to adults should be explored, that experiments should be freely initiated and that the results of these experiments should be kept constantly under review by regular reports from the head of the department to the Governors. The first effect of the appointment has been that the department has doubled its size in less than three years. It now consists of classes in French (with 35% of the department's enrolments); Italian (18%); Russian (begun in 1959 and already 16%); Spanish and German (about 8% each); and Celtic and classical languages (together about 14%), some 170 classes in all. It enrols annually about one-fifth of the Institute's 12,000 students, and holds one-third of its classes in the day (including short lunch-hour classes) and two-thirds in the evening. There are also regular series of study-tours and summer schools abroad.

The present account of the department's work is intended rather as a commentary than as a description: a series of reflections on the route that we are traversing, with some interim judgements about aims and methods in the present state of our experience, but certainly not a final prescription.

Certain traditional features of the Institute's work have borne upon the way in which the language department has developed. In the first place, large though the Institute is, it cannot cope with the number of students wanting to join, and every year considerable waiting lists are built up for vacancies in classes, particularly in the more popular languages (French and Italian). This is still true though the programme of the Institute is restricted to advanced courses. Beginners' classes are not offered in any of the modern European languages, and students are interviewed at enrolment in order to ensure that they have an adequate background in the language before embarking on any of the classes. The standard is described as that of 'O' level in GCE, but obviously this is not literally applicable to people over the age of twenty-five.

Secondly, the terms of reference under which the literary institutes were established by the London County Council emphasize the need to concentrate on liberal and cultural studies. There is no question, therefore, of preparing people for examinations, and the general outlook in all the classes must be towards an appreciation of the culture of the country whose language is taught. But culture does not just mean palaces and ruins, or the products of a golden age of classical writers: it means, rather, the total range of assumptions and attitudes which characterize one nation and differentiate it from others. These attitudes are enshrined in the language and are taught to the nationals as they learn the language at their mother's knee.

The object of any liberal teaching of modern languages should be the imitation of this process and what we have set out to do is to seek ways of teaching foreign languages in this sense. It is an exercise in stimulating the imagination of the student, so that he becomes aware not only of forms of words in a foreign tongue but of the cultural attitudes that they imply: he becomes imaginatively aware of what it feels like to be a Frenchman, an Italian, a Russian.

Thirdly, arising from this, is the practice we follow of employing only native tutors. On this subject much can be said on both sides and it is as well to remember that country of origin is only one among possible qualifications to teach a language. Fortunately, London seems to have a supply of teachers who are native speakers of the language they teach. Before the principle could apply widely, however, pension and insurance problems might have to be eased to make possible a free interchange of trained people for longish periods. But our view, based on our experience, is that (other things being equal) the native tutor brings something to a class that we regard as valuable: he *is* a foreigner.

Given the competent[1] native teacher of broad human interests and experience, the student not only has the authentic accent in his ears; he will be as close as he can ever hope to be in a classroom to the real-life situations he is preparing to meet on his travels: the direct personal relationship of himself and the foreigner. The atmosphere is genuine and not artificial—at every turn of the discussion, moreover, he will come up against those unspoken assumptions which are part of the imaginative realization of a culture different from his own.

---

[1] *Competent* is a term that immediately calls for definition. Most of us would prefer a more precise adjective, like 'trained' or 'experienced', but where, at the present moment, can a prospective tutor gain the experience or training necessary for this particular branch of adult teaching? Some successful school and university teachers leap at the opportunities offered by our less formal atmosphere and less rigid syllabus and adapt themselves to the different type of student with joy and unerring good sense, but others find it extremely difficult to lay aside their normal routine at the end of a tiring day and to make the right adjustment of personality.

It is possible sometimes, though it is by no means a fair or reliable test, to try out the would-be new teacher as a substitute for a temporarily absent member of the staff. What we prefer to offer is a programme of understudy and brief teaching practice in the classes of our more experienced tutors, to be undertaken during the summer term before appointment, followed up by a seminar in the first year of service. Obviously something more intensive than this is needed, but at least in a large Institute like ours there is quite a range of individual abilities and the prospective teacher will fairly easily find a kindred spirit on which to model himself. We would willingly open these facilities to those from outside, particularly if some other major centres would be prepared to open their classrooms to visits as part of the project.

Fourthly, the teaching must derive from the common traditions of English adult education; namely that the work is an active partnership of tutor and students; that the syllabus and pace are dictated by the needs of the students in the particular class; that the students bring to the discussions their maturity and experience of life as the counterpart to the tutor's academic training; and that as questions of taste and value will therefore constantly arise, the tutor must give these full play while keeping clear the distinction between matters of opinion and matters of fact. A student's progress and standard are thus largely relative and not open to precise objective assessment.

Now this is not the tradition on which the teaching of foreign languages in England is normally based, and the textbooks and other aids are all directed towards the objective standards of examinations. Hence we have been forced into a complete reassessment of our language teaching and a quest for types of course which relate to the ascertained needs of adult students rather than to preconceptions based on school curricula; and a reassessment too, of what we mean by success in a liberal language course.

Over the last five years in this Institute we have seen a steady growth in the number of language classes and in students attending them—now about 2000 a week. What the figures do not show, however, is how far this is a measure of success in any but a purely administrative sense. A larger number of students staying a shorter time could mean more failures but—much the same statistically—could mean that more students had received sufficient help to progress on their own, with books, radio, travel and other methods. There is still much to be learnt about the measurement of success in language teaching; examination reform[1] will help no doubt, but for many reasons we do not wish to be limited in our activities by the strait-jacket of any test, however ideal.

---

[1] An interesting step forward in liberalizing the form of examinations is to be seen in the revised French paper of the LCC Certificate of Secondary Education.

All our students on first appearance must convince us that they have already taken 'O' level GCE, or pass a quick oral test from a GCE paper. So, in theory at least, they should be able to look up their own grammar, choose suitable books, find some interesting wireless programme, travel in their holidays. Some people do so, but since others fail to manage on their own, and since many indeed spend years in adult classes and never seem to grow wings and take flight, perhaps one may be allowed once more to attempt a brief assessment of the processes of language learning.

Language, being a means of communication, supposes two parties: the foreigner and yourself; the book- (or letter-) writer and the reader; the teacher and his student or class. At its best this is a very personal relationship. The ideal is clearly the one-to-one relationship, the suitable foreigner and yourself, meeting if possible in his country. Since this is rarely possible just when and for as long as we need it, we try other methods. In the early stages we would probably not choose the book-and-reader or broadcaster-and-listener relationship, just because these must be less personal and because communication should be a two-way process. Sooner or later we revert to the teacher-and-class solution—preferably the trained native teacher. However, for the very reason that classes often have to be too large and contain students of varying standards, and certainly of varying abilities and sense of urgency, manifold problems arise here.

How difficult to create in a classroom the ideal atmosphere where in the learner's imagination at least this feeling of the direct one-to-one relationship of the foreigner and yourself can survive: this is the human situation we try to meet when abroad. For free uninhibited expression in the foreigner-and-yourself relationship an atmosphere of equality is essential. Our school teachers and class books always seem to cultivate the habit of the teacher's asking the questions for the pupil to answer. Some of this is necessary, but it puts the learner into the 'second fiddle' position. (After months of *Shut the door, Smith ! Open the desk,*

Jones ! let the pupils tell their teacher what to open and shut and observe the increased interest!)

Any tourist soon discovers that it is usually he who needs to ask the questions in foreign lands, but it is surely common observation also in any language or social circle that it is an easier role in conversation for the shy person to ask the questions and to put the greater load of answering on to the older or more knowledgeable partner. In adult classes there is no justification for a tutor to appear as the 'senior' partner, but it is more important still that the lesson be a two-way process and the atmosphere one in which the students get substantial practice in questioning the tutor rather than the reverse.

It is fairly widely accepted now in the teacher training colleges that a child's experience with his mother-tongue must have some relevance to the learning of foreign languages. We agree that a child understands before he speaks and speaks a long time before he writes. Thanks to the present school examination system, the childlike enthusiasm is soon damped by a complete reversal of this process. In an institute of liberal education like ours, where students are specifically *not* prepared for examinations, there should be every opportunity for benefiting by the new approach.

It sounds easy enough: first—comprehension; second—speech; third—writing. We feel, however, that too often these are mistakenly interpreted as being divisions *in time.* They are surely 'horizontal' divisions tracing our path till the end of the road. At each lesson there should be something new, or harder, or faster in the foreign language to stretch our power of comprehension *to the full.*

Speech, though following comprehension, should not really begin later; it is merely the two-way development of comprehension; comprehension of the foreigner by me and then comprehension of me by the foreigner. It begins indeed in Lesson 1, we hope, with 'yes' and 'no'.

Writing too can start in Lesson 1—at least in certain languages —by the copying of words just being learnt. In this, however, we

D

are primarily fixing words and phrases visually in the memory. The great menace with the written language is still the shadow of examination which makes so many of us instinctively introduce *translation* into language teaching. Comprehension of the foreign tongue, we have indicated, is a basic necessity at each appropriate stage but translation has no real place in the art of individual communication between the foreigner and ourselves and indeed in adult life is a highly specialized profession.

The majority of textbooks—published as they are to capture the school and examination market—by emphasizing grammatical detail, *translation* and the study of short extracts from foreign novels ('unseens') lead the adult student ever further away from the simple principle above: that language is a communication between the foreigner and yourself—a two-way process of some intimacy.

The conventional school textbook does even more harm than this: it is not only too large and suggests to the adult student—with a mere one and a half hours a week perhaps—that he must battle on until every page is covered (though this might take several years), it tends to make him 'book-bound'—a high scorer in the sports dear to the 'best years of our life' such as putting sentences into the indefinite past—as if one ever did—but relatively helpless abroad when he meets the person he would like to talk with.

Incidentally, the course which is almost exclusively based on a grammar textbook runs the great risk—especially at times of inclement weather—of the student's making the very easy discovery that he might more comfortably be reading those same chapters at home. Where tutors use a more direct method, put more of their own life-experience and personality into the class and use comprehension and extempore conversation, the student has his attention—both eye and ear—focussed on the tutor and cannot find any substitute for this by staying at home.

To speak now of our own Institute—leaving aside the elementary students and those who for reasons good or bad have decided that 'A' level French, etc., is the sort of language they would fain learn—what policy is it that we feel should be followed in an adult centre of liberal studies?

We suggest boldly: Emancipate the student as quickly as possible! Put him as soon as we can into a position to manage on his own—whatever the effect on our statistics. If he is book-bound (tied, that is, to his grammar manual) free him! Show him how to use dictionary and grammar book for reference, by all means, but free him from his dependence on them. Despite the pleasure and self-flattery we find in the deep loyalty a student develops to his favourite tutors, still promote emancipation; by use of tape-recorder and gramophone, let him hear other native voices. The tape-recorded programme can not only bring authentic dialogue and drama into the classroom, it is excellent preparation for attuning the ear to the foreign radio, which is certainly an essential step towards emancipation. If the tutor is a man let the class hear women's voices and vice versa, certainly the voices of well-known authors and of people in the news.

'Emancipation', 'managing on one's own', is a process that should if possible be pushed through in two or at the most three years from 'O' level GCE. To do this in two years requires great perseverance on the part of the tutor, as he will constantly have to fight against his own instinct to strive for perfection; it is tempting to hold back the class while some struggle for a more correct pronunciation that they—with their advancing years—inwardly aspire to, or to allow grammatical corrections to damp the spontaneity of self-expression.

Of course, at 9 p.m. the tired adult will make grammatical mistakes. It is easy to trip up on an exercise of mixed past-participle agreements in French at this time of day—some of us will continue to do so for many years. Emancipation in our sense must, of course, be accompanied by *shortcomings* in one sphere or another. We tend to say: in one and a half hours a week perfection in all directions is impossible, it is good enough in the circumstances if the student can make himself readily understood by the foreigner and can grasp the gist of what the foreigner says—in class, on the street, on a tape, a broadcast or in book or newspaper. The past-participle agreement is nice but not usually essential to international understanding.

Listening, dictation, ear-training, reading (chiefly at home), conversation (by, not at, the student), lecturettes, all of these ingredients we supply—and more. The permitted size of such classes raises a problem for the administration: a conventional grammar class with translations, exercises, dictation—where the class works as one unit—is not greatly different from, say, a history lecture, it can cater for larger numbers of students. The type of class we have attempted to describe, with an essential content of individual student participation, cannot fully succeed if the average attendance is much more than a dozen.

The fear is sometimes felt by freelance tutors that such a policy of emancipation, if successful, would inevitably lead to lower numbers and the closure of classes. The old picture of loyal students faithfully following the same teacher (regardless of the grading of the class) for ten years or more has indeed its attraction for those dependent on this profession. What evidence we have, however, suggests that this is a false fear. Firstly, any success in helping people to stand on their own feet, to put the language to practical, independent use, will attract new students in greater numbers; secondly, emancipation, for a variety of reasons, creates new demands.

The *linguistically emancipated* student, whether from our own language classes or outside, will sooner or later have experienced the need for regular practice of the language. Books of the right difficulty and interest are comparatively easier to find than foreign broadcasts, for it is still difficult to obtain the detailed programmes of foreign stations. But books, like many broadcasts, are rather third-personal and students soon realize (as do indeed the non-native teachers of a language) that regular practice alone prevents rustiness and that practice needs two-way communication.

The challenge to an Institute like ours is to devise suitable recipes for this emancipated student. It is relatively easy to arrange for lectures on literature. This is already established in university extramural classes, but there—as too often inside the universities—the medium is frequently English; an obstacle is then placed between the student and the foreign language, and the class, instead of mastering the language with the literature, may find itself concentrating on the bald facts of literary history.

What is much more difficult is to find tutors who will run a literary working-party—as opposed to lectures—in the foreign language: a group where all will join in discussion, read a book a week at home and have some worthwhile comments to offer afterwards.

Sometimes, while building up the necessary clientele, it is worth trying a play-reading group, each time stepping up the comments and discussion, but here the availability of books is a problem. Adapted and annotated editions are expensive, the cheapest foreign edition often hard to obtain in sufficient quantity, and consequently a danger exists that a play, instead of being read at 'theatre' speed, will be made to last a month and even a term—that is, ruined as a play.

It is difficult enough to run a really advanced oral group without the 'old hands' monopolizing the tutor; it is harder to run a good *discussion* group about current affairs of the country concerned. The tutor needs to be an up-to-date native who is constantly in touch with his homeland and regularly revisits it. Even then a great deal of preparation is necessary, and often the tutor—if he is in contact with the right supply—will be tempted to revert to films and lose the one-to-one touch. Art, cinema, music and other background topics are suitable for 'emancipated' groups in the larger Institute, as, of course, the more obviously intelligent tourism—geographical and historical background. Again the problem is to develop student participation. Now that transparencies are widely collected, even by non-photographers, it is a popular procedure to let each student in turn give a five (at the most ten) minutes' prepared travelogue and to see that the other students ask the questions.

Many English students are naturally poor conversationalists

anyway, and it is difficult for them to be more loquacious in the foreign language than in their own. Not only must we help the student to ask questions off his own bat, we must show him how to talk—in an interesting fashion—about those interests, experiences, hobbies, which he would most naturally want to talk of to an English friend he has just met. An impersonal *explication de texte*, or an impartial survey of the French social services, are excellent in themselves but the Englishman abroad more often than not will need to say why some *English* author is worth reading, or tell someone what is good about our Health Service. Even at the more advanced stages we feel it is important to *harness* the material given on the foreign country to increasing the student's power of expressing views and opinions and experiences of his own. Conversation and discussion groups must face this dual need of communication: when abroad, the questions we mostly want to ask relate to the other country; the questions we would like to answer more fully usually relate to our own.

A conversation class must be *just as carefully prepared and integrated* into an overall plan for the year as any straight language class. The student must have a sure foundation to build on and a clear grasp of what he is expected to add to that building each time. Having been given a basic framework of the minimum grammar and skeleton phrases with which to ask questions and state information, he chiefly needs a definite procedure for adding vocabulary—a programme of subject headings to be covered during the year (leaving a few spaces in which to take advantage of topics which seem to have borne good fruit and could be expanded). He should be shown, if necessary, how to differentiate between 'essential vocabulary', for the finger-tips, 'useful vocabulary' which one should recognize at once though not always be able to use so readily at this stage, and 'low-priority vocabulary' which should *not* be allowed to clutter up the notebook. This last category will be large if the student is to concentrate properly on the others; he should have a clear idea of his own needs (hobbies, travel interest, social demands) and ruthlessly discard words and phrases which to his neighbour may seem important. The student's own experience of life must be allowed fullest expression.

Not only should the tutor refrain from overfeeding the student with low-priority vocabulary, he must provide, just as carefully as his grammar-class colleague, for the regular revision and re-employment of the 'essential vocabulary' so far given and always set the students certain tasks in preparation for the next lesson.

To emancipate the student we must also put him in a position to enjoy the sort of book he enjoys in English—this should happen within two years of 'O' level. Although it may not be possible to persuade students to read books of reputedly higher literary value in the foreign language than in their own, this may easily follow. More skilfully written novels and plays are often more worth while for vocabulary, more memorable and hence rewarding, often better constructed and therefore easier to follow.

For the student who has until now been fed solely on minute extracts contained in modern school textbooks, the discovery that a complete novel can be finished and enjoyed within weeks or less is often a revelation of such magnitude that he will step forward in confidence to new victories. Early victories are very necessary to success, so care must be taken at the outset to choose *short* texts with wide modern appeal and students must be helped towards quick reading largely at home, for the gist only (as with their own language) and not translating line for line with a dictionary. With some authors more than others, students should learn how to identify and skip the unessential and to follow the main thread so as to finish the story quickly.

The objective being an ever-greater amount of home reading, a major problem to be solved is the adequate provision of books. To begin with, the class must use the same book, otherwise there would be no time for other activities; later on, reading lists, class loan libraries and a volunteer class librarian will be needed. The sets of books must be readily available for frequent changing, otherwise they will be made to last too long and the whole object of the exercise lost. Individual books will need the most careful selection and grading.

At the outset, collections of short stories will perhaps be the most rewarding, because of the easier and more frequent opportunities offered for scoring a 'victory' over the language and because of their variety of human situations, vocabulary and style. To start a longer novel and then find that the reactions of the class have been misjudged and that interest cannot be maintained is a major defeat of enthusiasm. A simple routine in which each week a fresh story is begun in class but stopped at a psychological moment so that the student has to solve the mystery at home gives scope to new conversation each week and above all makes the class practically immune from any interruption of interest due to individual absences. Humorous stories should have some priority but good characterization and good action are the chief need—not, however, in the form of those boy adventure stories aimed at the school market! Since one finds in most collections of short stories at least one-third of the contents to be unsuitable either because, despite the name of the author, they are poor stories or because the style is too involved or the vocabulary too specialized, the problem of having sufficient reading material at hand remains very difficult.

Little research has been done on the use of the newer audio-visual aids for the advanced adult student and in any case few evening class centres can expect to have such equipment at present. The portable tape-recorder, however, is of great value to the language student—*every keen language student should have one at home!* Normally it is his only way of hearing how inadequate (or otherwise) is his own pronunciation; it is his best way of practising at home, enabling him to capture news items, broadcast lessons and suitable foreign programmes and repeating them till he has mastered the essentials. Some day, no doubt, students will expect to find facilities in the classroom for recording parts of their lessons to be used for revision at home; certainly even now, a library service of carefully graded revision-drill tapes would be a great help. We sometimes record shortened versions of stories studied in class to be used for recapitulation of vocabulary at a later date.

There are many more uses of the tape: its stimulus to a play-reading group and its use in introducing songs or the voices of writers, actors and so on are obvious, but its chief value may still be in attuning the ear to foreign radio which is one of the aims of 'emancipation'. And we must be careful to keep it as an aid, not an end, and to limit carefully its amount of class time (the enthusiast will often abuse this). Our general experience is that tape-recorders are used best by those tutors who have their own at home for the preparation of material and that these need to be matched to the machines in the college. Furthermore, the college itself needs at least *two* similar machines to allow for editing and for the transfer of items from one tape to another (without cutting) so that a carefully graded library of teaching tapes may be built up.

With one and a half hours a week as our normal instructional period, and dealing as we do with more advanced students, it is difficult to envisage a large place for work in a language laboratory. In the initial stages of language learning, especially where more than one lesson a week can be arranged, the advantages seem very obvious; a great deal of individual pronunciation, question-and-answer drill and grammar exercises can be performed, which in the normal class is extremely time-consuming and indeed boring for those who are awaiting their turn. We shall hope that in future most of our students will have had such a course before they reach us. However, while pleading for further research on the audio-visual needs of the advanced student, we venture to suggest that our aim here should still be to 'emancipate'. The film-plus-tape and sound-film side of the audio-visual technique should be developed, with clear diction, of course, but at ever greater speeds, until the student is ready for the commercial film. Films of 'background' interest are needed as material for class discussion. The conversation and grammar drill, however, that is often a part of audio-visual technique has either served its purpose before the period of emancipation is

D*

under way or, we suggest, needs very careful exploration before application to advanced adults. The business gentleman of forty, or the enlightened lady of fifty-five, who have successfully found their way about abroad, not only may be rather averse to being drilled on standardized sentences, but—knowing their own very different interests only too clearly—need now a much more individual treatment, as we have mentioned above.

Above all, as a literary institute not handicapped by examination requirements, we are free to offer much more than graded courses of straight language and conversation. With double-banked classes each evening (from 6 to 7.30 and again from 7.30 to 9) the student can easily combine other activities with his language class: he may choose a debating group or a play-reading and discussion group, take his literature in serious or lighter vein, join a class where the homework is some piece of original written work in the foreign language (play reviews, book critiques, sociological topics, art commentaries—anything of general interest for discussion by his colleagues) or he may take a class where the spoken word only is used and he must address the class on some subject of his own. The student can take his own choice for a balanced diet.

Finally, the idea of emancipation must affect that beloved institution the trip abroad. Study-tours and residential schools are obviously valuable and rightly popular, but if they simply take the student about in a sealed package they may diminish rather than enlarge his freedom in the language. Hence in the foreign summer schools that we have arranged the object has been to lead the students to new starting points for their own exploration of the country's culture, by engaging individual students or small groups on projects of their own that took them away from the tutor's guiding hand; by balancing together the subjects of the different groups (art, archaeology, music, literature, language, for example) so that they might discover the resources of the neighbourhood by different routes; and by an appropriate choice of centre. (Recently we have been to Siena, Aix-en-Provence, Moscow, Leningrad, Tashkent and Samarkand.)

In emphasizing the personal relationship between tutor and student as the main factor in this policy of emancipation, and in stressing the contribution of the native teacher, we may have given the impression that all this can be left to the light of nature provided the tutor was born in the right place. In fact, of course, the success of this policy depends on its being shared by all the tutors engaged in it, and a good deal of regular consultation and discussion is inevitable, as well as the routine training in teaching methods that everyone needs. But it is certainly our experience that where the aim is shared and the students come to feel the freedom and relevance of their work in and out of the classroom, these language courses are among the most stimulating and rewarding of all forms of adult education.

6. Language-teaching for Extramural Students: An Experiment

ELIZABETH MONKHOUSE

WHILE language teaching to adults is an expanding field, it is one increasingly thoroughly tilled by various agencies. The entry of university extramural departments into the field requires some justification and the experiments carried out under the auspices of the Tutorial Classes Committee of the University of London in recent years was viewed with some initial misgivings both in the department and in the Ministry of Education.

The following account is based on the experience of four three-year tutorial classes and seven one-year sessional classes carried out by five tutors over the last seven years. While it draws mainly on two completed cycles of three years each taken by the same tutor, the experience of other tutors has been taken into account.

It is generally accepted that extramural departments are concerned with the kinds of liberal studies taught internally and that 'university standards' should be aimed at in extramural classes. The interpretation of this term is the subject of some controversy, but it is recognized that, while extramural students meeting once a week cannot cover the amount of ground attempted by full-time internal students, they should follow the same principles of disciplined study, should learn to read, analyse, appraise and marshal their own views in the same way. What they lack in academic background and breadth of study they make up, to some extent, in maturity of judgement and experience. This theory has worked out satisfactorily in such

disciplines as literature and history, but there have been difficulties in subjects which demand of students a certain basic
ground-work, such as mathematics, the lack of which has greatly
inhibited the teaching of physics or astronomy to adult students.
In the study of foreign civilizations there has been hitherto a
division of labour whereby the teaching of the language has
usually been in the hands of Local Education Authorities while
extramural departments have confined themselves to courses,
often very successful, on the history, economic and social systems,
politics and government of other countries or their contribution
to the arts, immediately accessible in music and painting,
available only through translation where literature is concerned.
An adult student wishing to study language at the same time has
usually had to shuttle between two classes, and any bearing the
one may have had on the other was purely fortuitous. In a few cases
the first part of the class-meeting was taken by an LEA language
teacher while the second part was taken by an extramural tutor
dealing with the civilization of the country. Apart from the
unfortunate implication that the one is inferior somehow to the
other—a theory borne out by the discrepancy in the rates of
remuneration of the tutors—this practice seems to be based upon
a misconception of the role of language which is an essential part
of the civilization of a country, which grows out of it and at the
same time influences it. Properly conducted, the study of
language is an effective medium for the study of the civilization
of a country, its historical roots, its national developments and
peculiarities, its values and traditions.

To separate the two is to lose an educational opportunity; to
combine them is difficult. Since extramural classes meet only
once a week it is clearly impossible for anyone starting a new
language to make enough progress, even in three years, to close
the gap between elementary language-work and adult liberal
studies in such a way as to make their juxtaposition meaningful.
It is therefore necessary, in extramural classes, to insist upon
some previous knowledge of the language, even if this is sketchy
or rusty. Since French is the first modern language taught in

British schools, this is the one in which the London experiment
has been carried out, but as the teaching of other languages
permeates our schools it should become possible to extend the
venture to German, Italian, Russian and other languages. How
to define the required starting level is difficult. As a guiding
principle, students with 'O' level French, or a more remote
School Certificate, have been encouraged to try the classes, but
some of those who reached this standard on paper proved unable
to follow the spoken language or to express themselves in it
while others, bereft of any paper qualification, had the temperament which enabled them to struggle through to meanings and
to make themselves understood. In the end it has proved more
satisfactory to apply a special test whereby students were required
to write answers in French to questions on an unseen passage of
French prose and then to try out their oral aptitude in class.

The basic method followed in the first two years has been one
of combined *lecture expliquée* and *explication de texte*. Every
student is provided weekly with a copy of a duplicated text in
French, sometimes a week in advance, sometimes unseen. The
passage is first read aloud, the students taking turns to read while
the others are asked to try to follow without looking at the text.
Correction of pronunciation, accent and phrasing is given the
degree of correction depending upon the degree of proficiency of
each student. A modicum of instruction in phonetics has been
found useful, particularly in correcting vowel-sounds, but as
perfection is not insisted upon, this study has not been carried
very far. Then, using French as the medium of instruction, the
class works through the passage sentence by sentence. Students
who do understand are invited to explain (in French) or put in
another context to show its meaning any word or expression not
understood by another student. This, of course, is one of the
ways in which the interests of students of different levels of
attainment are reconciled since all play a part, albeit a varying one,
in the exercise. The tutor supplements their efforts where need
be by further explanation or by pantomime. Every effort is made
to avoid the use of English, for the system is based upon the

cultivation of the habit of thinking in French rather than upon translation, which is, in fact, represented as being a treat only allowed at a more advanced stage. As words are introduced they are discussed first in the context of the passage and then in the more general context of French civilization. If the word *instituteur* occurs, for example, it will be set in the context of the *école primaire* or *cours complémentaire* and the *école normale primaire*, after which its relation will be shown to *le professeur*, *l'agrégé* and the *lycée* and the relative closeness of the latter to the university will be brought out. Derivations of words are a source of great interest, and adults to whom plain memory-work comes hard are more likely to remember the sense of *un goupillon* if they know about the fox's brush and the way in which the popularity of the *Roman de Renart* caused the supercession of the now obsolete *goupil* (in spite of the later borrowing of *vulpin*) by the current *renard*. Semantics are another source of interest. The evolution of words like *bourgeois* and *honnête* reflects the progress of social attitudes in the past, while some present-day slang is revealing about the present, as well as entertaining.

While vocabulary is a major preoccupation, grammar and syntax are not forgotten and points of both are raised in the text under examination. These, too, are usually taught in French, though occasionally an explanation is given in English if there seems to be a danger of misunderstanding. Since this language teaching is directed towards the end of understanding, grammatical exactitude is regarded as of less importance than, for example, the proper use of tenses. It is better that a student should get his verb in the right tense with an incorrect agreement than vice versa, for the latter means that he knows some grammar but the former means that he has some feeling for language. It is a question of some difficulty to determine how far correctness should be insisted upon. In general, the principle followed has been that no student shall be inhibited from saying what he wants to say. In the case of a weak student there should be only enough correction of the spoken word to make him generally intelligible, while the more advanced student is allowed less latitude. Where written work is concerned, more corrections are made because the inhibitions are less crippling, though here, too, the weak student should not be too discouragingly deluged in red ink, for the object of the exercise is, after all, the discussion of ideas.

These, then, are the principles of the linguistic approach, but every text is also the subject of a *lecture expliquée*. The language study, which forms the first part of a two-hour session, prepares the ground for the examination of the content. As fluency increases, less time is spent on the mechanics of language and more upon meaning, so that linguistic study merges into the discussion of ideas. Plainly, the choice of passages is of the utmost importance. Each one should be chosen to stretch the capacity of students without defeating them, and it should contain enough of the vocabulary required to be useful in developing the subject, though supplementation on the lines suggested above is always necessary. Above all, its content should be designed to introduce subject-matter worthy of discussion. The length of passage varies with its degree of difficulty, availability for preliminary study, the stage of the course and the nature of its content, from about 250 to 500 words. It has been suggested that there is room for the publication of a book of suitable passages. It is a superficially attractive idea but might well contain the seeds of its own destruction, for the essence of this approach is its liveliness and flexibility which might soon be lost if a selection of passages, however well chosen, were allowed to predetermine the shape of courses. It would be particularly cramping in its application to aspects of the contemporary scene which may come more tellingly and more à propos from the pages of *l'Esprit* or *le Monde* than from the literary passages which one is more inclined to enshrine in textbooks. Reflections on the cost of living or on a political crisis are valuable at the moment of publication and may lead to the discussion of broader issues, but when they have served their turn they should be discarded. Less obviously, the repeated use of tried favourites of a less ephemeral kind may lead to stereotyping and staleness.

If the justification for the entry of extramural departments into this field is that language is an essential part of civilization, the teaching of languages must be done in such a way as to lead to deeper understanding of that civilization. This depends partly upon the methods of which there has been some discussion above and partly upon the general content of the course. There is a long tradition of extramural courses based upon the history of other civilizations upon regional geography, upon comparative government, politics, sociology and economic systems. Courses in literature read in translation are not uncommon. Synthetic studies of the civilization of France or Germany, Italy or Russia have led to a more informed understanding of their peoples, to the appreciation of another set of values and assumptions, to the comprehension of other angles of vision. Where this has happened it has made a useful contribution to international understanding of a rational kind and to a general enrichment and broadening of interests. The language-teaching available to adults has, by contrast, often suffered from poverty of content. It is true that holiday travel and commercial contacts are on the whole unexacting in the demands they make for communication on the intellectual plane. The antics of M. and Mme Machin and their ineffable brood in Paris and at the seaside or the discussion of bills of lading meet these modest demands. But there is an appreciable number of people who need something more, who are looking for the kind of course on France or Italy or some other country which the extramural departments traditionally provide, *plus* the added dimension of language, which gives depth to the whole range of content. It must be recognized that the amount of ground which can be covered in a given period of time is less than would be covered in a course conducted in the mother-tongue. However, not only is the study of language on liberal lines a valuable form of learning in its own right, but there is reason to believe that the deeper understanding engendered through the added dimension of language makes for a more sustained interest and ultimately for a more prolonged study. There are a number of courses on France conducted in English and lasting for a single session; how many are there lasting longer than that?

There is, of course, no formula for the planning of courses of this kind, but one pattern successfully used has included a first year of history, a second year on the character of present-day France and a third year in which there has been an introduction to French thought and literature. There are obvious advantages from the point of view of content in starting with history which provides a good foundation for the two years following. From the point of view of language the choice is more debatable. The passages used have, in fact, been contemporary texts, translated into modern French where necessary. One of the first, for example, was an extract from the *Song of Roland* (in the Bédier translation) which, in addition to its dramatic quality, has the advantage of illustrating the relations between a feudal monarch and his barons. It contains some archaic constructions which slightly detract from its value as language teaching material, but even these can be turned to account in discussion of historical syntax, while changed meanings (e.g. *c'est votre homme*) launch an exercise in semantics. Some medieval writers (e.g. Joinville and Commines) have a simple style which, once translated, is very suitable for the early stages of the course, and the vocabulary is usually of the kind familiar to those building upon foundations of school French.

The history taught is not very systematic. It aims at providing on the one hand a broad outline and on the other some vivid impressions of atmosphere or of important events. Thus Joan of Arc's forthright letter to the King of England, proclaiming her intention of coming '*pour vous bouter hors de France*', may introduce the Hundred Years War. The Abbaye de Thélème gives a noble glimpse of Renaissance man and woman, introduces the sixteenth-century conception of *honnêteté* and reveals a side of Rabelais proof against traditional Anglo-Saxon sniggering. La Bruyère and Saint-Simon may represent the court of the Sun King while Bayle and Voltaire undermine reverence for the *status quo*. Rousseau introduces a new conception of the State, and with the Rights of Man modern France enters upon the scene. Napoleon I lectures his legislature on the importance of sound finance and Victor Hugo reduces Napoleon III to dwarf-size. Zola defends Dreyfus, Jules Romains recalls World War I and Bernanos or Blum recaptures the *malaise* of the thirties. On the *débâcle* of 1940 Marc Bloch gives a sober historian's eye-view of the disaster in which he was involved or Simone Weil supplies a devastating analysis in her study of *déracinement*. Such a selection has the advantage of providing a variety of styles and outlooks while preserving a sequence of events and some unity of subject-matter. Clearly these passages cannot by themselves provide all the material for even the barest outline of French history. They are supplemented firstly by brief explanations in class, secondly by the provision of books for private reading. Here the question arises: in what language should this be? Ideally, everything should be in French, but this must rarely be possible. In the first place, students, unless they are advanced, find two consecutive hours of grappling with a foreign language very tiring. In the second place, discussion is crippled if it has to proceed in the halting French of most adult students. It therefore seems preferable in such circumstances to make a clean break and conduct the second part of each class-meeting in English, at any rate to begin with. Later, French begins to encroach upon the second hour, but in the early stages it can only do so at the expense of the 'liberal content' of the course. Soon it is possible to give the historical background in French, after which questions and even discussion begin to come naturally in the same language. The tutor must be sensitive to the needs of the students, not only as between one group and another but also as between one evening and another with the same group. There is such a thing as collective fatigue, and this, or the particular difficulty of the subject under discussion, may necessitate an apparent retreat from the high-water mark of an earlier week. There is nothing to worry about in this. Flexibility and a relaxed attitude are necessary if the usual Anglo-Saxon linguistic cramps are to be overcome and as long as the mixture is not allowed to become too confusing, it is even possible to start in French, return to English if the students seem tired and, when they are rested, to go back to French in the same evening. It is untidy, but it works. In reading, too, the question arises as to how much should be done in French. Books in both French and English should be available. It is essential to have one or two short general histories (such as Charles Seignobos's *Histoire sincère de la nation française*) from which students may, if they wish, get a continuous outline, but few, at this stage, will read fast enough to enjoy full-length French history books. Most of their reading of background is still done in English and supplementary reading in French requires a great deal of guidance in the suggestion of chapters or even shorter passages which can be profitably read. Similarly, in the writing, which is a part of all tutorial class-work, the same problem arises. Few students are able to express their ideas adequately in French and it is therefore necessary at this stage to divide written exercises into two categories. In the one are the papers of the usual extramural class kind, written in English. In the other are exercises based on the text studied in class and the discussion arising out of it or on the reading undertaken in French, where the energies of the student are directed towards expressing in French ideas already explored. It must be confessed that the correction of this work, and of all free composition in French, is a very exacting task. It takes a great deal of time and calls for constant decisions as to how far to carry correction. It also calls for an immense amount of *written* explanation, for there is rarely time to explain more than a few of each student's mistakes to him orally, and they have all made different ones. But the effort put into the correction of written work is greatly appreciated by adult students, who enjoy the opportunity of expressing themselves freely and of trying out their ability to 'think in French'. Translation, as already mentioned, is used very sparingly and then as a means of exploring the meaning of some crucial passage in French whose subtleties are better understood as the result of an attempt to render them in one's mother-tongue. It is done as a private written exercise and discussed fully in class. Translation from English into French is not used at all. It is an admirable exercise for advanced students, but for those whose prime interest is to make themselves at home in another language it has the drawback of constantly pulling them back to thinking in English. There has been no pressure from students to introduce translation from English.

In passing in the second year from history to the study of France at the present time there is a move into actuality which comes at a good point in the linguistic development of most students. Many have been reading newspapers for some time and are ready to enlarge their knowledge of the economic, social and political realities which lie behind them. Vocabulary needs a good deal of enlarging at this stage, for while school French and the kind of private reading undertaken by intelligent adults provided much of what was needed in the first year, the literary-cum-historical character of our modern language teaching leaves yawning gaps in the requirements of the second. An intelligent Englishmen talking to a Frenchman is at least as likely to want to discuss the cost of living, the educational system or the election prospects as to discourse upon the Versailles of Louis XIV or the lyric verse of Victor Hugo. Yet he is equipped (after a fashion) for the latter and not at all for the former. Few graduates in French, after distinguishing between a *scrutin de liste* and a *scrutin d'arrondissement*, could go on to explain the niceties of *apparentement* or the joys of *panachage*, yet the electoral laws of France have had an important effect on parliamentary representation and thus upon the government of the country. Our neglect of the political and economic sides of French life and our tendency to dismiss them as 'too complicated' or 'not serious' have led to a lop-sided view of French civilization profoundly misleading and even dangerous. The down-to-earth attitudes of extramural students, who seem constitutionally adapted to asking awkward questions about what is going on, may prove a healthy corrective. The acquisition of the vocabulary associated with the contemporary scene leads at once to some questioning of the social and political assumptions which underlie it. What is the difference between *la bourgeoisie* and *les classes moyennes*? Where do *les cadres* belong in the industrial hierarchy? in the social hierarchy? Why are there three sets of initials (CGT, FO and CFTC) to correspond to our TUC? What is *remembrement* and what is its importance in the upheaval currently disturbing rural society? Who are the *bouilleurs de cru* and why are they in trouble? It must be admitted that it is hard to find tutors equipped to deal with this part of the syllabus and that the emphasis of several of the experimental courses has been more literary. But where tutors are prepared to acquire the necessary background and keep abreast of developments it has been of great interest. To the students the immediacy of the problems is a spur to self-expression and the wide range of material encourages the pursuit of personal interests. This, in turn, has led to the presentation of papers, prepared by students with individual help and guidance from the tutor, upon subjects of their choice. The experience has given confidence and is one of the factors in bringing about the linguistic 'great leap forward' which has marked the second year of three-year classes. Reading in French should by now be easier, and a higher proportion of the books provided should be in French. However, few of the books of adult content are adapted to the needs of the student whose language is still elementary. Students must soon move on from the easy general books by Maurois (*Portrait de la France, La France change de visage*) to the rigours of Morazé, Duverger or Fauvet with whom a good deal of guidance must still be given. Reading matter must still be provided in English both for the slow students and for those with limited time who wish to cover a good deal of ground. In writing, too, there is still room for papers in both English and French, the latter now embracing more ambitious subjects than in the first year and demanding the expression of more of the student's own views.

In the third year a different set of problems arises. Its aim is to effect an introduction to French literature through a selection of set books chosen by the group after long (and agonized) consultation with the tutor. The technique of studying whole works, as opposed to extrapolating the ideas contained in texts of a few hundred words, is, of course, quite different. From a good deal of floundering some principles have emerged clearly, though several problems remain unsolved.

The choice of works must be severely limited in both number and length in order that everyone should be sure of reading every set book. Eight works were found to be more than enough for the twenty-four-week period, though none of them was long. These were, by students' choice: *Le discours de la méthode* (Descartes), *Selected Pensées* (Pascal), *Phèdre* (Racine), *Tartuffe* (Moliere), *Un amour de Swann* (Proust), *La guerre de Troie n'aura pas lieu* (Giraudoux), *La peste* (Camus) and *Les séquestrés d'Altona* (Sartre).

The books should be available in cheap editions so that students can buy them and give them a first reading before the session opens. (This is possible in extramural classes where there is a close season between Easter, when the books are chosen for the following year, and the end of September.) There must be some insistence on the study of the texts, and the plan of study, especially the identification of any passages for special treatment, should be made clear in advance so that preparation can be properly directed. For supplementary reading other works by the chosen authors have been provided and some critical works, some of which were in French and some in English.

The choice of books is made on the basis of interest in authors, periods or particular subject-matter. Language study is now a matter of meaning and style. What do *géométrie* and *finesse* mean to Pascal? What do *essence* and *existence* mean to Sartre? What are the characteristics of the alexandrine and what texture do they give to the plays of Racine? Grammar and syntax still contribute something. Why does Thésée switch from *vous* to *tu* in his confrontation with Hippolyte in *Phèdre*? Why does Proust suddenly introduce a verb in the perfect tense after a series in the past historic in the famous passage about the little *madeleine*? But these are incidental now, means to the understanding of style.

The greatest problem at this stage, and one to which no solution has yet been found, is the difficulty of conducting a discussion *at this level* in French. In the second year much of the discussion is at a factual level and even matters of opinion are based on interpretation of facts which are not particularly difficult to assess if one has the necessary vocabulary and information. But the discussion of great works of literature and philosophy is taxing enough in one's own tongue and to all but the most fluent it is an impossibility in a foreign language. The choice lies therefore between selecting set-books so unambitious as to be discussable at a simple level in French (in other words, to sacrifice content to language study) and reading in French great works which must be discussed mainly in English. Some students have expressed regret at this apparently retrograde step but recognize that once-a-week students can hardly expect to tackle what is beyond most full-time students. All are glad to use French for the preliminaries—details of the author's life and time, placing of the work in its background—and equally glad to use English to discuss the meaning of the *Discours de la méthode* or *Les séquestrés d'Altona*. Their choice has been unhesitatingly for the great works, since, having so little time, they cannot afford to waste it on the second-rate.

This, then, is the experiment which has been carried out in the London area during the last few years. It has been limited in part by the requirements laid down for the students, and it is noteworthy that classes have been held in such culturally well-heeled centres as Guildford, Ealing, Finchley and, of course, central London. It is to be hoped that experiments now proceeding in primary and secondary schools will later provide a much larger reservoir of potential extramural students in a number of languages. Even more has the experiment been limited by the requirements laid down for tutors. They must speak fluently and without accent and at the same time be ready to work through the halting and sometimes excruciating efforts of their students. They must be equipped with the scholarship in depth which their university training has given them, but be prepared to extend their study far beyond the existing scope of university modern language departments. The experiment has justified itself. In spite of all the blunders and disappointments by which all such attempts are attended it has given a number of students an informed view of France and a will to carry their inquiry further. One of the tests of success has been the bearing of parties of students who have visited France as a supplement to their class work. Their active enjoyment has borne witness to the effectiveness of their unorthodox preparation. Perhaps the flower of it was seen in the comment of a third-year student emerging from a Sorbonne professor's lecture on *Phèdre*: '*Très bien, mais pour moi il ne donnait pas assez de poids au jansénisme de Racine.*'

7. Vocational and Non-vocational Work in Institutes of Further Education

O. EISNER

IN the following observations, an attempt is made to set forth, without too much generalization, the main problems facing language tutors and organizers of language courses in institutes of further education. Comments are also offered on the value of some of the work being done at the present time.

Institutes of further education form part of the provision classified by the Ministry of Education as 'vocational'. Where modern languages are concerned there is in fact little work with adults that is of a truly vocational nature, most of the teaching being directed towards students whose aims in attending language courses are not connected with the acquisition of qualifications. However, the primary function of the institutions in question (notably technical and commercial colleges and colleges of commerce) is clearly to serve vocational ends. This, then, is the aspect which will be dealt with first.

I

Vocational courses

The classification of courses into vocational and non-vocational corresponds broadly with the further distinction made between full-time courses, taking place during the day, and part-time work, usually but not always in the evening.

In most institutions the following *full-time* courses will be offered during the day:

100

1. Secretarial courses (two years) in commercial subjects, shorthand and typewriting, which also include up to four hours a week of instruction in French and one other foreign language (German or Spanish). Exceptions apart, the best that can be attained in German and Spanish is a standard considerably below 'O' level. More, perhaps, can be expected in French.

As the students concerned are for the most part adolescents completing their full-time education, it is unnecessary for us to consider them further.

2. Shorter 'intensive' secretarial courses (two terms) for graduates and older students possessing fairly high qualifications. Here results are better. Students show more interest; they often have posts in mind where some knowledge of the language studied will be of positive value to them; they have an intelligent approach to the subject, and at the end of the course they are very well prepared for continuing the study of the language with profit.

3. 'Sandwich' courses leading to a Higher National Diploma and for which employers release students during three successive years for two terms per session. These include the study of one foreign language and are very much our concern here since they raise a number of fundamental problems.

The remaining full-time work, as far as languages are concerned, consists of university entrance courses and, in some colleges, of preparation for external degrees. Important enough in themselves, they are not peculiar to institutes of further education and will not be considered.

In technical colleges which offer courses leading to an external B Sc., a 'scientific' foreign language is often required, but since this plays a comparatively minor part in the B Sc. examination, no great importance is usually attached to it.

As for the *part-time* work in institutes of further education, classes with a vocational bias are now regularly arranged to meet the needs of specialist groups such as business executives, civil servants, scientists and technologists. They often take place during the day or they may be divided between daytime and evening. Short, full-time, intensive courses serving the same type of student are also not uncommon and are likely to increase in number with the spread of audio-visual equipment.

The problem of organizing suitable courses for these specialist groups is basically the same as the problem to be faced in the sandwich course, namely that of devising a restricted syllabus which concentrates on teaching a specialized form of the language. But in practice it is in many ways easier to answer the needs of the out-and-out specialist than to determine the exact nature of the restricted form of the language which will best fit into the general framework of a sandwich course.

The scientist who wishes merely to read foreign language publications in his own field can, for instance, acquire such proficiency as is needed for the purpose in less time, perhaps, than he needs for acquiring the scientific variety of his own language. For in order to grasp a scientific text in the foreign language the knowledge of his particular scientific subject is much more important and helpful than a profound knowledge of the foreign language as such. The principle of hearing–speaking–reading–writing will, in his case, have to be applied in part only. A good grounding—even in the old-fashioned way—in structure and forms, some practice in which '*la plume de ma tante*' is replaced by patterns in the vocabulary of whatever scientific discipline happens to be his, should enable him to read the papers which interest him with only a little more difficulty than his native colleague.[1] Thus in Russian a standard of proficiency defined as sufficient to enable a scientist to 'make sense of a Russian scientific paper' has been reached in forty-five hours

[1] More often than not his knowledge of structure and forms may help him, without too great or systematic an effort, to branch out into the living language. In fact, courses specially designed for scientist and technologists, designed, that is, with a bias towards scientific vocabulary, have a tendency to fade out, and members of such courses turn up again in 'ordinary' language classes where they feel they may acquire the framework for their special vocabulary more easily and quickly than by bothering with a representative number of texts some of which, owing to the high degree of specialization in the sciences, may be nearly as little comprehensible to them as to the non-scientist.

of intensive tuition, and considerably higher standards in 200 hours (cf. C. W. Hanson, *The Foreign Language Barrier in Science and Technology*, ASLIB, 1962).

The sandwich course consists of a number of disciplines trimmed and adapted to meet the presumed needs of adults in various walks of life. In addition, an even more rigorously curtailed form of a foreign language is deemed desirable. If its provision presents tutors and organizers with difficulties this is for certain identifiable reasons.

In the first place, directives contained in reports of studies touching on the matter are vague and rather superficial. A few cursory paragraphs in the MacMeeking Report, which deals at length with the many problems of *Further Education for Commerce*, yield the following references, in all of which the terminology will be seen to be of a general character, devoid of detail.

Thus, (a) 'vocabulary and content (should be) specially selected for commercial needs', (b) courses 'should last about six months', (c) with regard to 'languages studied as optional subjects in advanced Sandwich Courses in Commercial subjects' ... 'Students should be obliged to reach the required standard ...', (d) background knowledge such as 'commercial conditions, business practice and social customs of the countries concerned' (three quite extensive and specialized fields not automatically covered during the training of a teacher of modern languages) should be included.

If they are meant seriously these are high, praiseworthy aims. So high are they that only a numerous well-qualified staff could attain them, and even then it would probably prove impossible.

The result of objectives such as these being placed before those responsible for the more specifically vocational aspect of sandwich courses is the kind of lip-service which is all too common when liberal arts subjects are inserted as 'cultural background' into technical training.

For instance, it is agreed that the amount of the language to be taught must be restricted. But the other aspect of specialization —namely, that what is not whittled away should be studied all the more profoundly along selected lines—is often ignored. On one occasion when the writer tried to obtain a clearer explanation of the standard to be aimed at in the foreign language part of a sandwich course the reply given by those under whose aegis the main, non-language sections of the syllabus fell was a vague hope that the students would (after three six-month sessions in three successive years!) be able to exchange simple courtesies with foreign visitors or hosts.

Another example of the same attitude is that although an examination in the foreign language is included as a matter of form at the end of the completed course, success or failure in it may have no connection with success or failure in the course as a whole. This fact may be discovered more or less accidentally by the person responsible for devising and teaching the language classes; it is certainly not unknown for the students to be aware of it before the tutor is.

A further difficulty arises when it comes to finding suitable teaching staff. Language departments, like many others, depend very largely upon the services of part-time personnel, quite often native speakers who are not usually qualified language teachers, let alone experts in commerce, science and technology. Their sense of responsibility may be great enough, but it is by no means certain that they either know what their actual duties are or how to discharge them.

When a qualified, full-time tutor is in charge other drawbacks make themselves felt. As a rule, the course occupies no more than about a fifth (or less) of his teaching commitments and important though he recognizes a sandwich course to be, the fact remains that it is concerned with beginners. Thus, even when his timetable permits him to prepare his lectures, he will naturally put beginners' classes lowest on his list of priorities. Yet sandwich courses, as we have seen, are precisely those that call for planning, research and thorough preparation.

And so it all boils down to a humdrum language course at the tail-end of a curriculum, the rest of which, whether it is better taught or not, presumably lends itself more readily to adaptation and compression, and certainly appears more immediately useful to the student himself.

The attitude of the student is indeed crucial in the matter. Attendance at language classes is compulsory, and this, to him, is a not infrequent source of regret. Why so little enthusiasm, even nowadays? As Section 17 of the Annan Report (on the teaching of Russian) points out: 'linguists may fear that their chances of promotion (in industry and commerce) will be slight unless they are trained to do the main work of the organisation to which they belong . . .'. Which is another way of saying that students in vocational courses are not given enough practical incentive when expected to learn languages. Attainment of any other professional qualification can often be a great advantage to a career, but being a linguist (a translator, an interpreter, a foreign language correspondent) is hardly ever regarded as belonging to a profession. Nor can the financial rewards enjoyed by linguists provide much encouragement. On the contrary, the accomplishment, once acquired, leads nowhere in particular, and of this the reluctant student is instinctively aware.

Finally, there is the manner in which integration of language instruction into the rest of the vocational course takes place. At present the periods of language study are sprinkled through the timetable, not always at the most propitious times. Concentration, the value of which for language teaching became so clear in the crash courses conducted during the last war, is lacking. A case might well be made for accumulating the hours of language work at the beginning or end (or both) of the sandwich course, no other subject being studied for a week or two. The result would be a greater sense of purpose and undoubtedly better results.

All this does not mean that every effort is ineffective or that no results at all are achieved in the language part of sandwich courses. Waste and frustration there are, however, and these cannot be overlooked.

One of the points made in the Annan Report (Sections 110–13) is this country's need for an institution of the order of the

Dolmetscherschule, which in Germany and Switzerland offers training in modern languages by specialist teachers who are particularly qualified to deal with fields such as economics, commerce and technology (*see* footnote on p. 107).

One result of the establishment of such a language institute or even of the incorporation of some of its characteristics into existing institutions would be the eventual elimination of most of the problems touched on so far. Not only would the study of modern languages become an end in itself instead of being thrown for good measure into vocational courses which are better without it but all students attending classes would be genuinely interested in the subject. In addition, aims and methods would be more clearly defined and research into them co-ordinated; the use of available teachers, including the native speaker, would be properly organized; short intensive residential courses would be available; there would be a more rational system of examinations.

The highly successful *Ulpan* method used in Israel for teaching Hebrew to new immigrants probably also has lessons for us, with its comparatively short but intensive courses, which may be fully residential, and which plunge the student immediately into those aspects of the living language with which he will be directly concerned.

It is perhaps not without significance that the Annan Report makes no mention of existing British institutions in its tentative suggestions for a 'language institute'. The outlook of examining bodies, as manifested in some of their examination papers (*see* Appendices I and II), is such that any assistance from these quarters in attempts at revolutionizing or reforming existing methods of teaching and testing can be ruled out.

II

Non-vocational courses

As has already been said, teaching for specified ends represents only a subsidiary aspect of work with adults in institutes of further education.

There is a majority of part-time learners whose purposes are not well defined. When the question of aims is raised at all they declare they 'just want to learn the language'. Such students are by and large accommodated in evening classes. In the bigger towns there is usually a sufficient number of native speakers of the foreign language who offer their part-time services,[1] but a good deal of evening work is also left to full-time staff.

Language teaching to adults like these takes place under conditions quite different from teaching in vocational courses proper. Problems of method are of a different order but they are no less difficult to solve.

The greater part of the faculty of native speech consists in the exercise of deeply ingrained habits, mental and physical. Some of these habits have to be overcome and others exploited when a new set of habits is to be acquired. Habits are acquired by constant repetition. Learning by repetition becomes less and less pleasant as an individual matures. Other ways of learning, learning by association and learning by forming concepts, are much more acceptable to the adult. But the memorizing of a basic set of several hundred phrases and sentences is an indispensable first step in a foreign language. Particularly with adults, repetition can be made more palatable in the guise of variety; and more opportunities, perhaps, than with very young people can be seized for inductively arriving at general principles, abstractions: that is, relieving sheer drill by *the discovery of grammar*. The discovery of grammar, not its imposition. The most obvious way of contriving such discovery is practising with sentences the meaning of which is changed while their pattern remains constant, an exercise analogous to paraphrasing where the words and

[1] The essence of a certain kind of foreign language teaching has been enshrined once and for all in '. . . those stupendous Russian ladies who, without having had any formal training at all, manage somehow, by dint of intuition, loquacity, and a kind of maternal bounce, to infuse a magic knowledge of their difficult and beautiful tongue into groups of innocent-eyed students in an atmosphere of Mother-Volga songs, red caviare, and tea.' V. Nabokov: *Pnin*).

E

sentence patterns change while the meaning remains more or less constant.[1]

We should expect that every method adopted will endeavour to select *vocabulary on the basis of frequency*. ('God willing' in the second lesson of a widely used beginner's book for German is, alas, not an isolated example.) Nevertheless, the value of frequency word counts for language learning is not unlimited. Targets like '800 words in so-and-so many weeks' are naturally based on frequency. But 800 words are not learnt by learning 800 words but by encountering them with greater frequency than other words among at least three times as many. Some half of those surplus words will be retained as 'passive' vocabulary; the rest will be partly lost and partly more easily acquired than such as have never been encountered before. This passive vocabulary is an invaluable asset, and the fact that it is, indeed, acquired without great conscious effort can be very well exploited. Very many people who expose themselves regularly to commercials on television acquire a body of soap-powder poetry, of the music that goes with it and of maxims in lapidary prose on milk, petrol, toothpaste and what-not. Here we cannot possibly speak of their having 'learnt' the texts and tunes in the sense in which we habitually use the term 'to learn'. It may be said and it may be sad that people are thus successfully exposed to what may often amount to harmful brainwashing. But the obvious capacity of the brain to be washed can be turned to much less objectionable ends.

Phrases which form the small coin of *everyday speech* must be taught as soon as possible, irrespective of the fact that most of them are highly idiomatic, or contain forms which, in systematic presentations of grammar, are usually dealt with at the end.

Even the *history of the language*, a purely academic line of research, can be profitably exploited for language learning; in particular, the study of German offers innumerable opportunities

---

[1] Pattern changed (paraphrase): Leave the room . . . Get out.
  Pattern constant: I have read a good book lately.
            I have had a good breakfast this morning.
            I have written a long letter today.

for using, for instance, Grimm's Laws, the sound shifts, for acquiring and retaining new vocabulary. As for the Romance languages, an intelligent person can often understand at once most of what he hears or reads in French, Italian or Spanish because of the Latin–French stock of English vocabulary. And even the Slav languages show, up to a point, features that remind one usefully of the fact that they, too, belong to the Indo-European family: *Mother–matyeri, daughter–docheri, son–syn; water–voda, fire–ogon'–ignire, bread–loaf–khlyep–golova (head); woman–zhena–kin–gune–genus–* ... *know–ken–znat'; prosit'–precare–pray; town–gorod–hortus–garden; the numbers.*

Drawing the attention of students in such directions may not have any direct effects but it certainly makes them more watchful and receptive for relationships of that nature. When encountering new words on the page, but often also when hearing them, students whose attention, just occasionally and by the way, has been drawn to facts like these, will very often make the right guesses, save time and emancipate themselves to some degree from the dictionary that so often retaliates when not handled with the discretion it deserves.

Recently, great stress has been put on the oral-auditory nature of speech, and the too early use of *books and writing* has been deplored. On the other hand, it is very difficult for a grown-up person to forego an aid to the memory which he rightly believes to be indispensable in so many ways. It is even possible to exploit this understandable eagerness to have things in black and white. The teacher can, for instance, open the first lesson by dictating material, without of course giving any hints on spelling. Excellent results can be achieved that way. We get almost perfect pronunciation in the first lesson. The exceptions are, of course, phonemes altogether alien to the native language. Here and not only here,[1] the results of descriptive analysis can and must be applied in practice. The teacher, even the native teacher, who is unaware of the possibility of explaining an alien phoneme and

[1] See A. E. Darbyshire: 'Literacy of scientists and teachers of English', *Nature*, No. 4895 (24 August 1963).

thus helping the student acquire it, simply produces his own speech, makes the student repeat it, hoping for the best, and then gives up and says (but is not always sure) that it will come 'with practice'. It may and it may not. And the practice cannot but result in fortifying the student in whatever form his mispronunciation takes.

A foreign language teacher must be able to instruct the student how to form *alien phonemes*. Sometimes, often even, trial and error may lead to success, but precise description often saves hours of practice. An example from German: the frontal *ch* as it occurs in *ich, brechen, Küche, Köche*, etc., is a sound very difficult to produce for most English students. It is, to give it its full descriptive name, an unvoiced palatal spirant in which the middle of the tongue is raised against the highest part of the palate, and as such it is nothing but the unvoiced form of the non-syllabic semi-vowel sonant j as in Yes, Youth, baY, etc. The terminology does not matter in this context, but the analysis it reflects must be known to the teacher, and it is up to his ingenuity to convey this analysis effectively to the student.

Another old-established routine that has recently been under attack is the practice of *prose translation*. All the arguments brought against it are sound. It is true that the routine into which prose translation tends to degenerate does not teach speech, does not greatly increase vocabulary, does not even teach 'grammar' efficiently. Should it be abandoned? Certainly, if it is practised in such a way that it serves no purpose, if, in Bloomfield's words, it '(keeps alive) the eighteenth-century scheme of pseudo-grammatical doctrine and puzzle-solving translation . . . solving puzzles is not language-learning . . .'.

And yet it should not be abandoned.

Many students, perhaps a majority, do actually want to acquire the skill of translation. This is a legitimate desire, and of great practical importance in industry and commerce. Further, it is true that we cannot expect prose translating to provide practice in speaking. Only speaking can do that. But a certain way of tackling proses may even help in this direction. Prose translation, practised as it should be, can and should lead to valuable memorizing (and speech) exercises: it can provide, as hardly anything else can, great insight into semantic relationships; it may increase vocabulary slightly and familiarity with usages considerably; it may really and truly 'discipline the mind' in the way in which it is claimed, so often and so pathetically, by Classics masters—all this it can do, provided it is practised not as a dull routine chore but with ever new passionate love.

Finally, and this is not the least important aspect of prose translation,—the process of translating is a true model of the very act of 'finding words', of trying to 'express oneself'. But while the 'self' requires introspection to be known (and this may well offer very little to be expressed), the original, with all the faults it may show, challenges and offers itself to the student as an external entity for exploration, attack and conquest. Operating a few prose translations may often teach the advanced student by practice what he might not have the time or desire to get out of abstruse theoretical works on language.

III

But whatever the method, even with bad methods, inadequate teachers, inferior textbooks and other drawbacks, after a year or so most adult students can be expected to some degree to be able to follow, even in the new language, Cato's advice of *Rem tene, verba sequentur*. Many can now sit for first examinations as arranged by various examining bodies. It is at this stage that often up to half the number of such beginners give up. Why? It is not just those who have found it beyond them that become 'wastage'. Apart from all sorts of external reasons like marriage, change of residence etc., only at this late stage the student who has with such comparative frivolity 'taken up' the language a few months earlier lays it down again as he becomes aware of the question 'What for?'. Those who do go on with it must have found some answer to that question. And it is this answer which should be discovered and used for formulating the aim of non-vocational foreign-language teaching to adults.

At present many establishments of further education regard languages as subjects where results, *examination results*, should be attained just as in the other subjects they are catering for. But the middle-aged student does not, as a rule, seek professional qualification, or, indeed, any practical end, in studying the foreign language. Many do not even go abroad, apart, perhaps, from a fortnight's holiday not necessarily to the country whose language they study. This, naturally, applies particularly to Russian. Their contacts, if any, with native speakers of the foreign language are few and rare. They abhor examinations, although they do quite well in them after having yielded to persuasion and pressure.

But what is even more significant there is that quite considerable number of devotees who keep coming for years without making any appreciable progress or having great hopes of ever making any. In such cases the study of foreign languages appears by its nature to be an activity; an activity that is an aim in itself, like art classes, chess, folk-dancing, drama—a recreation. Amateur pursuits of all sorts are often idle, wasteful pursuits, selfish perhaps, particularly when viewed by ratepayers who have never been seized by any such passion. The question here is not whether such pursuits should be encouraged and supported or not. It might be a good thing to face the fact that adult language learning is predominantly of this character and to adjust teaching and administration accordingly.

This *amateur attitude*, an attitude which provides pleasure for little effort and leaves the amateur content with such a kind of pleasure, may be harmful in many ways; but if we are frank about it we shall admit that in our time of specialization a full life consists in being a specialist in one way and an amateur in a hundred others.

What, then, is the use or value of this particular kind of amateurism, or, at least, what can, what might, it be? Such activity is certainly of value, more so, perhaps, than all other pastimes, hobbies and non-physical sports. Above all, this activity creates in the devotee what one might call linguistic consciousness and conscience, a state of mind which is not only necessary for learning a foreign language but which offers a wealth of new intellectual experience—a pleasurable state of mind.

This linguistic awareness, the creation of the habit of looking over one's own and the next man's shoulder when speaking or writing, of doubting, hesitating, selecting, the acquiring of a taste for the *mot juste*, the habit of thinking before speaking—all this makes for a certain amount of sophistication replacing a certain amount of spontaneity. This is the price civilization has to pay. And this is in many, and no doubt the best, students of a foreign language the result of their concern with language at a more advanced stage. If he called a spade a spade before he started out, this was because he didn't know better. If he calls a spade a spade now, this is because after long study he has learnt that it is the *mot juste*.

This is no little achievement: speaking with care is a sometimes embarrassing necessity for the person who is not quite at home in the language he uses. Such care may often be transferred to the use of his own language—a process akin to distantiation: the familiar made to appear unfamiliar.

Those who have reached in their studies a stage high enough for them to penetrate into the interior of the language where it is most characteristic of itself in its difficulty, in its beauty, in its profundity—such students may now be prepared to reap their reward in the form of a kind of study of poetry that is possible only to the bilingual person. The foreign language has been acquired to such an extent now that the superficial comprehension of the text presents no difficulties. But, thanks to 'alienation', the native language, which is superficially so well known, has a new ring now when approached in the way in which one has learnt to approach the foreign language: the native tongue revives, and it is as though it were heard for the first time. Any word taken out of its accustomed environment, say, the utterance 'Hurry up please, it's time' will, by mere repetition, be deprived of all its familiarity sooner or later. It will lose or gain in meaning, or change it; it will change its specific weight, as it were; it will become odd—as does happen with this very phrase in the pub scene in *The Waste Land*.

Such heightening of awareness is of value, as all heightening of awareness is. And what, after all, is the sublime use of language by the poet but such awareness? Not very many poets are not also translators at one time or another, or in some aspects or other of their work. Translators in a wider sense perhaps than the customary one. For the poet translates from the incommunicable into the communicable. And the user of his work translates from the poet's form.

And that is where the student of language and languages comes near an achievement denied to most monolingual persons. For, once the language student fully comprehends the untranslatability of what the beginner could easily construe (as is often so sadly done in examination papers); once the student understands a line in the foreign language so completely that he cannot bring himself to put it into his own; once he has reached that stage where despair and delight have become inseparable and indistinguishable—he has reached the goal which he was unable to define when he set out upon the adventure. He may not have known that he would arrive where he did and he may still be unable to describe it easily (just because he has learnt to speak with difficulty), but further education will have done what it should do: further education.

Note on the Sprachen-und-Dolmetscher-Institut, Munich

Languages Taught: English, French, Spanish, Italian, Russian—either as main or subsidiary subjects; one of each is usual. Students from *all* departments also attend (a) a set of lectures in German (some of them optional) with titles such as 'Economic and Political Questions of Topical Interest', 'Introduction to the Study of Language', 'Principles of Law' and 'Introduction to Technology', and (b) the *language laboratory*, used for recording students' voices, for concentration and interpreting exercises and for receiving foreign broadcasts (e.g. BBC). The laboratory possesses a 'listening library' of recorded and taped plays and other literary texts. Conference interpreters use it for simultaneous interpretation exercises.

Length of Course Main language: six semesters (three academic sessions). Subsidiary language: four semesters.

Programme Each course is sub-divided into lectures and exercises, both in part optional according to whether students wish to specialize in A. Economics, Law and Politics, or B. Technology and Science. Thus, for English as a main subject there are (i) *21 lectures in English* on subjects like The Commonwealth, Business Practice (three levels), Foreign Trade, Economic Geography, Technical and Biological Terminology, Elementary Physics and Chemistry, Government and Constitutions, Legal Terms, Characteristics of the American Language, British History, and English Literature; (ii) *Exercises* in oral expression, dictation, grammar, and translation, to which, in the course of the first four 'General Language' semesters, the following are gradually added: one hour per week's translation into German of an article from the *Observer* and a second hour's reading and discussion of passages from it; rehearsed and impromptu speaking; play-reading; commercial correspondence; practice dialogues for interpreters; translation of economic texts from and into English and German; exercises based on the lectures in Business Practice or those on Foreign Trade (optional according to specialization). The last two 'Special Language' semesters add essay-writing, consecutive interpreting, reporting and précis-writing (all compulsory) and *either* A. German political texts, the *Süddeutsche Zeitung*, English political texts, economic and financial texts, advanced course in economics and finance, seminar for Anglo-American and German legal terminology, translation of documents, commercial law and court interpreting; *or* B. Mechanical engineering, visits to works (terminology), interpreting, translation of scientific texts into English. Students taking English as a subsidiary subject follow the syllabus of the four 'General Language' semesters, including the Business Course and commercial correspondence.

Summary Allowing for timetable considerations and optional lectures and exercises, the weekly programme of a full-time student preparing for the diploma would include: Main language: 5–7 hours of lectures; 20 hours of exercises (including the laboratory). Subsidiary language: 4–6 hours of lectures; 3–7 hours of exercises.

8. Textbooks: The Present Situation

P. H. HARGREAVES

THE three main groups into which modern language classes for adults fall—vocational courses catering for a small minority, courses with aural and audio-visual aids for a growing number of business executives, and 'general interest' courses—all present special textbook problems.

On the whole, vocational courses fare best, since their needs correspond to some extent with those of upper classes in the schools, whose problems are roughly similar. A good sixth-form book is usually adequate for students preparing for the higher levels of the non-GCE examination boards (*see* Appendix I), any obvious deficiencies being remedied by the teacher. Such specialist books as *German for Scientists* may also profitably be used by adults. Unfortunately, there is a dearth of good specialist books.

The textbook demands of laboratory courses are manifold. Books are needed to assist and to augment audio-visual courses and also to supply material from which they can be developed. Each book should, preferably, be constructed for a limited purpose—to prepare, to accompany or to consolidate, as the case may be; there is no room for the multi-purpose book. Moreover, such is the rapid development of laboratory courses that in the near future the basic price of a 'textbook' may well have to include the cost of tapes and filmstrips, the book itself being unobtainable without them.

The difficulties inherent in the 'general interest' courses are well known. To begin with, in institutes of further education the naming of the classes is misleading. Principally in order to establish a pay-rate for the teacher, administrators use labels like: GCE 1st Year, RSA Advanced, Institute of Linguists

Final, and so on. These names have some relevance to the aims and ambitions of a tiny minority of the students, but unfortunately most teachers, out of a misplaced sense of duty, tend to ignore this fact and follow the syllabus. The administrators responsible for prescribing courses are rarely modern languages specialists and are therefore unable to give advice and guidance to teachers. They are also often unaware of the exciting possibilities of the work. The teachers concerned are all too frequently amateurs having little or no contact with modern theories and developments. As a result they often teach in what they consider to be the 'grammar school' way. They are confronted with an unsatisfactory teaching situation and, because of a lack of training, indifference on the part of administrators, or ignorance of how to effect changes, they struggle unsuccessfully to maintain interest and make progress. They rarely come into contact with publishers' representatives or see a comprehensive range of catalogues, rarely choose textbooks themselves or obtain permission to change them.

These three groups cover the majority of courses available in institutes of further education (including all grades of technical colleges). Statistically and factually we know very little about the students involved—which is possibly why so little constructive work is done on their behalf and why amateurism is so widespread.[1] There is also, unfortunately, no common meeting ground for administrators, teachers, students, examining bodies and publishers. Each one paddles his own canoe.

When we turn to the existing textbook situation we find a matching state of confusion. Approximately forty publishers are producing about 120 new books every year, apart from imported books for which no figures are available. In addition there are, of course, previously published books which are still in print. Thus, at any given moment there is such an embarrassingly large choice of books dealing with a relatively small range of subjects that the majority of teachers find it overwhelming and are at a loss to know how to take advantage of it. The new and

[1] See *Introduction* for a contribution to this field of study.

uninitiated must rely on tradition or hearsay or else make a virtually random choice from among a few readily available inspection copies.

Fortunately, a partial solution to this problem is in sight. In January 1961 the Modern Language Association undertook to survey some aspects of language teaching in further education, and one result was the setting up of a textbook sub-committee. This committee aims at producing a guide to as many as possible of those books that were available up to the end of 1961. Subsequent editions are envisaged. The extent of the problem involved can be gauged by the number of books received from publishers as a first instalment—over 200. At its meeting in March 1963 the sub-committee finally decided on the form that the guide would take. It is as follows:

```
TITLE:
AUTHOR:
PUBLISHER:
No. of PAGES:
No. of CHAPTERS (or 'lessons' if so called):
FORMAT:
YEAR—first published:                    last edition:
PRICE:
BINDING:
SIZE of printer's TYPE:
    (for German texts, state whether Roman or Gothic)
ILLUSTRATIONS—number:
    type (e.g. line drawings, photographs, etc.):
    relevance:
READING MATTER amount:
                    type of content:
No. of TENSES:
EXERCISES—type (e.g. completion, translation into French, etc.):
ANY GRAMMAR SUMMARY?
VOCABULARY CONTENT?
ANY END—VOCABULARY LIST?
If so, type (e.g. French–English):
    No. of headwords in each section:
GENERAL COMMENT or ASSESSMENT:
```

The advantages of a guide set out in this way are obvious, provided that it is comprehensive and as up-to-date as printing schedules allow. Details can be obtained from The Honorary Secretary, The Modern Language Association, 2 Manchester Square, London, W.1. It is to be hoped that the guide will highlight deficiencies in the textbook field and thereby exert some influence over future developments.

At the moment the two biggest obstacles in the way of scientifically produced textbooks are time and money. There is often a delay of eighteen months to two years between the completion of a MS and its publication, which means that the latest book published can be out of date in many important respects. Laboratories may well have the advantage here, as tapes are often produced in three months or less.

Royalties to authors are ridiculously low and discourage many potentially excellent contributors from entering a field where amateurism is rampant. Many authors, in fact, write from motives that have nothing to do with money. The student gains financially but loses in the long run by having books which nullify educationally sound methods of teaching and learning.

The biggest impetus towards the production of good textbooks is coming at the moment from the development of teaching machines. Research into programmed learning and its remarkably successful application have led some publishers to experiment with new types of textbooks, and the interest that these have aroused augurs well for the future.

Up to the present it has not been economically possible to produce textbooks of this nature that have been tried out, revised, tried out again, etc., on a group of learners large enough to be significant. Nor has it been economically possible to produce many books having a limited aim, a deficiency all too obvious from a perusal of publishers' blurbs, which often claim that a book can teach many aspects of a subject to many grades and levels of students.

There are indications, however, that a more enlightened era is coming. Our educational deficiencies are so glaring that any suggestion of a botched up repair job will be laughed out of court. Publishers, if they are wise, will move with the times and learn how to produce good books quickly at a price that will give a true indication of their worth. To achieve this they must make a united effort to find out exactly what is needed and then create the conditions that will enable the demand to be satisfied. One publisher is offering for sale a language course that costs £2000. Is this an act of courage or a sign of the times?

9. Teaching Languages for Specific Purposes

JOHN LOWE and MARGARET LOWE

I. The British Army

The organization in the United Kingdom that has had most experience of teaching languages to adults for a specific purpose is the British Army. It therefore seems appropriate in a symposium of this kind to make some reference to its aims, problems and methods. The following account is based upon information kindly supplied by officers of the Royal Army Educational Corps. Naturally, no reference has been made to classified material.

The Army is called upon to arrange training in foreign languages in order to meet three standing requirements. In the first place it is necessary to have on call a permanent quota of serving officers who, between them, can muster competence in the major languages of the world. The linguists in question are required to be thoroughly versed in the language or languages in which they have specialized. To take an example, there are always available at least a few officers who are completely fluent in Serbo-Croat.

Secondly, it is necessary to ensure that those officers and other ranks who are seconded to service with the armed forces of other countries should have at least a colloquial grasp of the native language. Thus, for instance, Army personnel on active service in the area of the Persian Gulf must be able to carry on a conversation in Arabic.

Finally, it is sometimes advisable that all ranks should have at least a rudimentary knowledge of the language of countries in which they happen to be stationed. At the present time troops based in Western Germany are encouraged to have some acquaintance with German in order that misunderstandings with German citizens should not arise through a simple inability to communicate.

Responsibility for fulfilling these three needs rests with the Royal Army Educational Corps (RAEC), although the Corps is not necessarily obliged to provide the actual training and there is co-operation with outside bodies. Thus, the cadre of experts of all arms is kept up to strength by sending selected personnel annually to universities. Those who are to learn Chinese or Japanese, for instance, become students at the School of Oriental and African Studies, University of London, or at the University of Hong Kong. A tour of 'language duty' in the country where the relevant language is spoken follows, usually for six months, but it may even last two years, during which time the officer is relieved of all other duties except that of mastering the language. Then, his period abroad over, every effort is made to post him to an establishment where he will be able to continue practising the language. Thus if he has learnt Thai he may be posted as military attaché in Thailand. Only by so thorough and costly a training does the Army believe it possible to obtain linguists of the calibre it requires.

Languages such as French, German, Italian and Spanish do not come into this scheme, since the Army can already draw on personnel with the requisite qualifications. For Chinese and Japanese the training is reckoned to last three years and to cost £4000 per student, exclusive of pay and allowances. For Russian eighteen months of intensive work is prescribed, incorporating six months' language duty. Intensive courses in Russian are regularly given at a language school permanently maintained by the Educational Corps at Beaconsfield in the United Kingdom. Other Army language schools exist for (1) German—at Hohne in Western Germany; (2) Arabic—in Aden; (3) Malay—in Singapore. Before describing how they set about their tasks it is useful to take note of certain principles which underly the Army's approach to the general problem of teaching foreign languages to adults.

(1) The Army, as a matter of principle, demands efficiency and quick results. Even so, its method of submitting its cadre of experts to a long and expensive training illustrates that, whatever the newspapers may have reported, the Army does not subscribe to the view that expertise in a foreign language is communicable at speed through short intensive courses and so-called revolutionary new methods.

(2) The Army is entirely opposed to the notion that there are natural linguists. Indeed, it is the opinion of those instructors interviewed that any soldier who has reasonable intelligence can be taught a foreign language and even that there is a firm correlation between a man's IQ and his ability in this direction. One instructor, with experience of organizing language training in several countries, had concluded that the qualities principally demanded in anyone willing to learn a foreign language were nothing more than intelligence and a capacity for hard work.

In Army courses the students are indeed expected to work hard. The five and a half hours in the classroom, followed by two further hours of private preparation, required at the Singapore school are an indication of the general attitude. At the Army school in Beaconsfield a forty-hour week is normal. The system was independently described by individual instructors from the two schools in such terms as 'no dead wood is tolerated' and 'we either make or break'.

(3) It is recognized that the major obstacle to be overcome in the Anglo-Saxon faced with learning a language is his self-consciousness. A desire to inculcate confidence at the earliest possible time is therefore the factor which governs all decisions regarding the size of classes (twelve is considered the ideal), the use of the spoken language (usually from the outset), and reliance on methods such as the short talk or lecturette given by each student in turn.

(4) A proper motivation towards learning foreign languages is also usually lacking in the Englishman. There is, therefore, a belief that all language students should be volunteers and, in fact, more volunteers regularly come forward than there is room for in

F

the schools. In addition, incentives are provided in the form of a system of rewards, not through an increase in salary but by means of a lump sum received on completion of the course.

(5) While remaining sceptical of the exaggerated claims made for audio-visual equipment, particularly in the United States, the Army does keep abreast of up-to-date thinking on the subject of language teaching. The first language laboratory was installed at Sandhurst and others are now being set up at Beaconsfield school and elsewhere. They are welcomed chiefly on account of their great value for repetitive work and their help in reducing self-consciousness. The guiding principle is that eight booths should be the maximum; the teacher must constantly be present and can never be dispensed with; self-monitoring is not only useless but dangerous.

Tape-recorders, film and other aids have in any case long been in use in Army training, although not as part of a laboratory.

(6) The Army tradition with regard to the choice of teachers has usually been to favour the native speaker. Nowadays, in general, the two-tutor system is preferred: that is to say, a minimum of formal grammar given by British instructors, supplemented by conversation with native speakers. The Beaconsfield school has always chiefly relied on former White Russians, who, when they retire, may be difficult to replace. On the other hand, the latter are very much bound by established routine and are often—understandably—resistant to new techniques.

(7) In all languages correct pronunciation is regarded as essential from the beginning. As a rule it is assumed that this may be acquired through constant imitation, but instructors are at liberty to use descriptive phonetics if they so wish. In Russian correct stress is also insisted upon from the outset. After six months (eight hours daily, five days a week) absolute accuracy is expected.

One further consideration which guides military authorities in their choice of syllabus is the Army's special problem of re-settlement. Personnel need to retire from the Service with, if possible, a qualification which fits them for civilian life. Language training is therefore directed towards two external examinations, the Civil Service Interpreters' Examination (taken by those who will work in the Army as interpreters) and the Civil Service Linguists' Examination (taken by personnel who will serve as instructors). There is, however, a strong feeling that both examinations need to be brought up to date. Interpreters, in particular, are woefully served in this country, and there is regret at the lack of a nationally recognized qualification. Even outside bodies capable of helping to train interpreters are not easily to be found.

Bearing in mind these guiding principles and special needs, it is interesting to look more closely at the work carried out in the Army schools. Here we shall take cognizance of some further features of the long, intensive course in Russian which is well established at Beaconsfield and of the short course in Malay which the Singapore school has also been running successfully for a number of years.

At Beaconsfield students are resident for twelve months, in principle using the foreign language outside as well as inside instruction hours, although the presence at the school of Army personnel not studying languages can be a considerable hindrance. In this respect the Combined Services school which was confined to the study of languages, and which did such sterling work during the war, was preferable.

Except for three short periods of leave (about two weeks in each case), the twelve months are entirely given up to working on the language, study periods taking up forty hours each week. Students may be officers or other ranks and are preferred young; thirty-five is felt to be the age limit. All are volunteers, specially selected according to criteria which were not divulged but which did not include any special tests of linguistic aptitude.

Methods of instruction are not stereotyped but are subject to change and experiment. Tape-recordings and filmstrips are made on the spot and undergo constant improvement and revision. No textbook had been found adequate without being supplemented by the school's own material. The history of testing at Beaconsfield would seem to show that students prefer regular tests along conventional lines which furnish them with guides to their own progress. Those whose progress is unsatisfactory are not permitted to continue.

It is perhaps the short intensive Army course which is particularly germane to the national problem of educating adults. The course in Malay given at the training school in Singapore lasts for five weeks and is designed for soldiers who will be working with Malayans and so will need to be able to communicate in Malay. It is not necessarily residential and no special qualification are demanded of would-be candidates other than a willingness to learn.

The Malayan language, with its straight-forward syntax and limited vocabulary, lends itself particularly well to the use of the direct method, which for inflected languages such as German or Russian is not invariably used by Army instructors. Thus, from the moment the course begins, the student starts to speak Malay and the instructor often gives instructions in Malay so that the student has the maximum opportunity of listening to the language. Vocabulary is increased daily by committing to memory a fixed quota of new words, bringing the total by the end of the course to a minimum of 800. This is not high (the Shell centre in London teaches 2000 words of the closely related Bahasa Indonesian in the course of one single month's work in the laboratory). But at the same time close attention is given to colloquial skills. Ear-training and comprehension are regarded as highly important, especially recognition of Malay stresses. Outside the classroom students are encouraged to listen in to the local radio and to eavesdrop on conversations among Malays. Towards the end of the course six Malay informants are brought into the classroom on several occasions and each one converses with two of the students.

The Army Colloquial Test which may follow short intensive courses is open to any officer or man asking for it, whether or not he has received formal instruction. This also applies to German, for which a target of 1500 words in five weeks is set, and to Arabic, for which, however, twelve weeks are required to reach a similar standard. In all three languages the vocabulary selected is partly military but basically civilian.

RAEC language instructors appear purposeful and aware of their very real achievements. They regret, however, that for administrative and financial reasons the supply of equipment must inevitably lag behind thinking. There seems little doubt that the creation of a national school of foreign languages would receive support from the Army.

II. Industry and Commerce[1]

It was more than anything else the realization that British industry needed linguists and was having difficulty in finding them that made the question of how we teach languages to adults in this country a public talking point and an issue in the national Press. The trouble, industrialists will tell you, is not that one needs foreign languages to buy abroad, for would-be sellers use English as they use the languages of most countries in which they hope to find markets. It is when trying to sell that a command of foreign languages becomes essential. In any case, the whole

[1] The material used in this chapter is derived from four main sources; (a) the answers supplied by a number of well-known companies to a questionnaire sent out by the editors; (b) personal interviews with education and personnel officers; (c) the FBI report; *Foreign Languages in Industry: Report of a Working Party*; (d) the writer's own experience of devising and conducting courses for business men in the Liverpool area during the period Easter 1962–October 1963. The following firms were especially helpful in supplying information: Richard Thomas and Baldwins Ltd. (Mr. J. Baker); Shell Petroleum (Mr. P. R. Chorley); Littlewoods Mail Order Stores Ltd. (Mr. R. C. Duke); Unilever Ltd. (Mr. J. Brosgall and Mr. F. Tyson); The British Aluminium Co. Ltd. (Mr. F. Liebesny); The English Electric Co. Ltd. (Mr. E. R. L. Lewis); Pilkington Bros. Ltd., St. Helen's (Mr. L. S. Newton); Imperial Chemical Industries Ltd. (Mr. C. W. North); Reed Paper Group (Mr. R. Robinson); The United Steel Companies Ltd. (Mr. R. Sewell); British Insulated Callender's Cables Ltd. (Mr. N.G. Treloar); Whiteley, Lang and Neill Ltd. (Mr. E. Whiteley). We are also indebted to the Institute of Directors for a description of work in its language laboratory.

trend of industry nowadays is towards international collaboration as never before; the language barrier must be overcome.[1]

So urgent was the problem felt to be in 1960 that the Federation of British Industries set up a working party, under the chairmanship of Mr. P. J. C. Perry,[2] to study not only the adequacy of the means available to train linguists for industry but also 'to what extent interest in the study of foreign languages should be stimulated'. The terms of reference were sufficiently wide to make its report, published in June 1962, an important source of information concerning the teaching of modern languages in general in this country and its conclusions have a bearing on far more than the specific needs of industry and commerce.

Thus, besides enjoining industrialists to aim at higher standards of translation, up-to-date advertising material, the preparation of technical glossaries, etc., the report also made recommendations relative to the national system of education. When looked at closely these may be seen to call for two lines of action: in the first place for what can be described as long-term measures—expansion at both ends of the established school curriculum, the setting up of a national language institute and of nationally recognized qualifications for testing practical proficiency, and, secondly, for immediate measures, to some extent of a stop-gap nature. These were (a) that technical and commercial colleges should provide intensive *ad hoc* courses aiming at fluency, using modern methods and catering for small numbers of students at times convenient to their work, and (b) that provision for the more specialized training of qualified linguists should be made within industry itself. The languages most needed commercially seemed to be German, French and Spanish, with Russian, Italian and Portuguese growing in importance. Chinese and the African languages must also not be neglected for the future.

It is necessarily the second group of recommendations which

[1] *Times Educational Supplement*, July 1963. See L. S. Newton.
[2] Mr. Perry is the director and secretary of the British Association for Industrial and Commercial Education.

must concern us here, since it is to their implementation that we must look for any immediate contribution to the problems of industry and commerce. The introduction of French into a few primary schools, encouraging though it is, scratches only the surface of the deficiencies pointed out by the report in the teaching of languages in the schools.

On the face of it there has been no shortage within industry and commerce of reactions to the emergency. Two firms—*Shell* and the *Steel Company of Wales*—possess their own language laboratories and a third has been set up by the *Institute of Directors*. Companies release their staff for courses in ever-increasing numbers. The failure of the Common Market negotiations, for a short time a great fillip to interest in language classes, made little difference in the long run. A circular sent out by Shell in the summer of 1963 asked for applications from staff in the London area who wished to learn a foreign language. Five hundred and fifty people took up the suggestion, a most encouraging response in principle but no small problem for the officer charged with satisfying the demand, the size of which may be appreciated when it is known that over three and a half years the Shell centre had dealt with 350 people and that another large company which is active in the field doubted whether over five years more than 120 individuals had undertaken some form of language training, including those who had followed gramophone courses.

A glance at details of some of the work being done in industry is instructive and appears to justify the following generalizations:

1. Each company or section of a large company deals separately with its own problems. Head Office usually has no details of arrangements made in subsidiary establishments and even in companies such as ICI, with many years' experience in the field, there are no uniform courses. It is therefore difficult to get hold of exact statistics. The principle, if any, is to satisfy local needs according to local resources. 'At present, language training in this Company lacks any real shape' is a typical comment.

2. *The emphasis is on experiment* and expediency. Firms are ready to try any method offered to them that may reasonably be

expected to produce results. Three large companies, with subsidiaries spread over the United Kingdom, will serve as illustrations. Thus:

(a) In one company, at a given moment, one man had just attended a three weeks' course in German for British business men in Munich, another was about to spend a term at Cambridge studying Russian, six more were attending evening classes in French, Spanish and Italian at different centres in London. About thirty people a year in the whole company followed gramophone courses—supplemented in only one branch by instruction from a local grammar school master; there was a plan to second sales personnel to agents on the Continent and one works had established a residential course in German for two separated weeks, the first in the spring, the second in the autumn, for men nominated to go to Germany under an exchange scheme. The appointment of local teachers to give instruction to groups of managers and others was being considered in one branch of the Company; another branch was on the point of sending personnel to Ealing Technical College. The Company also arranged short residential courses in German, taught by traditional methods, and prepared ten senior apprentices for an exchange scheme with a company in Dortmund.

(b) A company having a headquarters and something like twenty establishments, and needing to employ the languages of most parts of the world, was collaborating in various places with one university extramural department, several private language schools and a number of technical colleges. Some staff being transferred abroad had been sent full-time for a period of up to three months to a private language school in London. Although not possessing a language laboratory, the Company had found it necessary to devise its own courses on tapes for languages like Nepalese, the students monitoring themselves with occasional visits from a tutor.

(c) In the London sections of an international firm an average of forty managers a year borrowed sets of well-known language course recordings for French, Spanish, German, Dutch, Italian,

Swedish, Danish, Portuguese, and Russian from the Company. (It had been noted that the greatest wear was on the first two out of the ten records of the set.) For managers going abroad individual tuition was usually provided: ten managers per year received tuition in French, German and Dutch arranged by the translations department; outside teachers were provided for languages such as Spanish, Portuguese and Indonesian. A German conversation group had met weekly for three years, with an average attendance of twelve people; a French group of twelve chemists was about to embark on its second year: both groups were led by native speakers already employed by the firm. An investigation of the question of language laboratory tuition was going on and if a 'real need' were shown to exist a pilot scheme might be considered.

Other experiments described by various firms, large and small, included: 'informal social methods such as language lunches'; sherry parties attended by a few professional linguists—recommended as a way of testing practical proficiency or the success of a course; residential courses in a hotel with all conversation in the foreign language—reduced four weeks' intensive work to three, but exhausted the teacher; short films, e.g. a two-minute scene showing an Eastern bazaar to stimulate vocabulary queries; classes (sometimes voluntary, sometimes obligatory) held after or during office hours with a privately engaged tutor—in one well-established case three courses per year for the same group of students, each course consisting of eight to twelve weekly sessions, usually two hours a week with written homework; in another experimental case, three hours a week with written homework for two ten-week terms, followed by division into two conversation groups of one and a half hours each for a third term; use of classes offered by the French and Italian institutes; collaboration with Berlitz schools in London and Manchester; releasing staff for (a) two afternoons a week, and (b) every afternoon of alternate weeks for intensive courses—usually ten weeks long; other variants of the same approach.

3. *French and German head the list of languages taught* and

French is the favourite with students. In one research firm, which introduced courses in French, German and Russian, only French persisted; in a large provincial works French outlasted German and is still going strong for a third year.

When it comes to arranging classes in non-European languages companies almost always have to fall back on their own resources (as for Nepalese mentioned above), devising their own tapes, finding and training their own teachers. Mr. P. R. Chorley's successful pioneering course in Indonesian at the Shell language laboratory in London has been running since May 1960, under the direction of a naturalized Dutchman, recruited from the firm's branch at The Hague, where instruction in seven languages is already well established. (Five languages are taught in London.)

Curiously enough, once a competent teacher is found, the less familiar languages such as Malay, Hindustani and Nepalese do not offer as much difficulty as the most commonly known European languages. For instance, it is generally recognized that there must be a rigorous paring down to essentials of the linguistic material to be taught—in nothing is the need for research more important. With European languages, after very elementary stages, it has been found that nothing is more difficult either.

The German or Scandinavian or French business emissary will be found capable of holding forth in English on very many topics that his English counterpart will also wish to talk about in the foreign language. Courses of all kinds, whether in classroom or laboratory, must provide them with the wherewithal to do this if they are to be found satisfactory.[1] As far as accent is

[1] Some theorists of the language laboratory (Marty, for instance) recommend suppression of the 'discussion' as a means of teaching for practical ends, but whether this is desirable with business executives in this country, 'practical' though their approach may be, is a very moot point. The social aspect of the visit to the Continent, whether by technical representative or sales manager, is extremely important. Engineers, consultants, can manage to make themselves understood in factory or works with a modicum of knowledge; it is over a meal in the evening, they will tell you, that confidence is shaken. Thus, they need and demand help for such occasions. In a French class, an engineer, responsible for the direction of two machine-tool factories, had heard *La Peste* by Albert Camus highly praised both by business acquain-

concerned, too, few languages are found to offer more difficulty than the one most English people know or apparently want to know, namely French. Here, descriptive phonetics can be a most satisfactory aid.

4. *Standards*. Most companies do not recommend tests at the end of a course, on the grounds that the average student is already highly self-critical and will in any case underestimate his achievement. Encouragement is therefore preferred. A few firms holding a different opinion have, in the absence of a suitable national examining body, devised their own tests, set their own standards and even instituted a system of rewards. In at least two further cases, as far as our knowledge goes, the Institute of Linguists is used.

5. *Teachers*. Large international firms can usually recruit teachers within their own organization. Others encounter difficulties. The general view seems to correspond with that of the Army: namely, that two instructors per intensive course is the ideal—a trained British linguist to deal with grammar and special difficulties and a native speaker to improve accent and idiomatic usage. One firm, which runs its own courses in German and Italian, expressed an outright preference for native speakers, with the comment that 'equivalent British linguists are expensive and difficult to obtain'. For European languages Shell had come to the conclusion that university-trained British linguists were more effective than untrained native speakers, to whom students were apt to begin teaching English. The native speaker was also frequently found to be too tolerant of an inferior accent.

Where technical equipment was available teachers in general were said to show enthusiasm and considerable eagerness to

tances in France and by his teacher in this country. After twelve weeks' revision, he began to read the book, and the class discussion which followed provided a useful introduction to a new field of vocabulary. This is unlikely to be an isolated example. Politics and the French Constitution are particular favourites. Only the up-to-date will satisfy and the better students soon start reading a newspaper or weekly magazine in the foreign language, even if it is not also used in class.

experiment, the amount of the financial reward offered to them being apparently a secondary consideration. Among students, a tendency to rely hopefully on self-monitoring with gramophone records was observed and this was not confined to firms which were only just beginning to think about the problems of language training. Firms with experience of up-to-date equipment recognized that more, not fewer, teachers will be required if it is to be used to real advantage.

6. *Attitude towards audio-visual aids*. As one would expect, there is nearly always interest in and often a desire to benefit from audio-visual aids, indeed an assumption that courses involving them are necessarily superior, usually on the grounds that time is saved, self-consciousness banished and a better accent produced. Thus one description of a successful course run on traditional lines was qualified by the remark 'given by a particularly gifted teacher'. Firms often possess tape-recorders and even films. Many devise their own tapes.

At the language laboratory in Shell House, where the simultaneous use of sound and film had not been judged successful, the introduction of a television set into each of the eight booths was being planned. These would be used in the first place to permit the student to listen to outside broadcasts but chiefly so that the teacher might build up his own film and project it on to individual screens. In the near future students would be answering the television as they now answer a taped lesson. Time would again be saved.

Most firms, however large, find it more difficult to justify even a conventional language laboratory. It is perhaps important to treat the activities of international enterprises such as Shell as exceptional. On the other hand, Unilever, no less international, was still exploring the need for language laboratory work in the late summer of 1963.

7. In spite of the excellent work being done at Ealing, Holborn and elsewhere there is widespread dissatisfaction with *the classes provided by commercial and technical colleges* on the following grounds:

(a) Timetables and planning are too rigid. The recommendations made in the FBI report that courses should be held at times convenient to industry are not always heeded.

(b) Not enough of them possess audio-visual equipment.

(c) Where equipment is available teachers have usually received no real training in its use and seem to be expected to know immediately how to manage it. In at least one case they were required to produce their own tapes for French, German and Spanish at once, instead of being more reasonably provided with those already on the market so that they might experiment (in the absence of a national training scheme).

(d) What equipment there is is frequently faulty.

(e) As far as the ordinary evening class is concerned, the pace is said to be too slow to satisfy professional needs. Where crash programmes are arranged there are, however, complaints that they are too concentrated—e.g. at one centre a course in German requiring five hours a day, five days a week for six weeks was found to move too fast. When a full-time intensive course was offered in a major industrial centre there was only one enrolment.

(f) When classes were laid on specially, e.g. twice a week, partly in the firm's time, students of different levels found themselves together (this, admittedly, is frequently the students' own fault); syllabuses paying lip service to 'new methods' turned out to be traditional classes based on old textbooks. One book used in what was nevertheless a successful French course mentioned Susanne Lenglen as a promising tennis star. (Here the blame lies with the publishers who had just issued a 'revised' edition.)

(g) The place of the 'continuation' course needs careful attention—for keeping up as well as improving knowledge. Where there is no demand from the students for continuation a change of teacher or method is probably indicated. What the reasonably advanced student needs particularly are comprehension exercises—tapes of broadcasts, extended passages of the spoken language, which may be played and replayed, slowed down, discussed. It is not enough to urge a busy man to listen unassisted to foreign radio programmes and, once he has attained a certain degree of self-expression, to train his ear by himself. This aspect of language training for executives has, perhaps understandably, been overlooked in face of the need to impart basic essentials which first had to be dealt with. But in the case of the main European languages—French, German, Spanish, and Italian—and particularly in the case of French, it is important. So many prospective students have *some* knowledge of French or German or both, which they have almost never learnt to use to advantage. Turning latent knowledge into active knowledge should be recognized as an important aim deserving some study. 'Going back to the beginning' wastes time and discourages many a potential enthusiast. In this respect the use of tests to grade students from the outset seems to some justifiable and this has been adopted by the Institute of Directors. A generous financial policy with regard to numbers would seem essential.

8. *Private language schools* or 'consultants' are very often used, especially as their timetables are more flexible and they are inclined to be more co-operative. No great enthusiasm was encountered, however—in one case, results were described as 'not very convincing'. Enterprise and a desire to provide a commercial answer to a pressing need are clearly not sufficient in the present emergency. The problems of effective language training are too complicated and the real answers too costly.

9. *The students.* The average age of students is between twenty-five and forty but men of fifty-five and sixty are not unknown. They are salesmen and sales managers, production managers, engineers, technical representatives, junior and middle executives in stock controlling, management research, technical services, sales promotion, etc., with a sprinkling of accountants, industrial representatives, company secretaries, personnel officers and managing directors. When they are going abroad for any length of time their wives may be encouraged to learn the language too.

Learners can be divided into two groups:

(a) those having an *immediate day to day need* for the purpose of visiting foreign countries;

(b) those having an undefined need arising from their future prospects as executives.

It is in the case of the first group that one of the major problems which beset the whole business of language training in industry makes itself felt.

'*The people who most need training in a foreign language are often those whom it is most difficult to release*', comments *RTB*. And in answer to insistence from theoretician and teacher alike that a valuable course must be intensive, requiring the release of the student for several consecutive weeks, *Littlewoods* of Liverpool (who have devised their own programme and set their own standards) offer the following judgment: '*Experts will not face the facts of industrial life.*' There are 'firms which *cannot* spare executives for more than a few hours a week'.

Short of employing, at great cost, private tutors within the firm to fit instruction and practice into the rest of the executive's busy life (and this would not necessarily be an answer to the problem of intensive instruction) there seems no way out of this impasse. Thus the hopeful executive eagerly borrowing a gramophone-record course to be listened to in the morning while he shaves or some evening when he has an odd moment is easily explained, together with the proliferation of 'tutors' of dubious merit on all the bookstalls. Yet the truth, probably, is that in the end any solution must depend upon the attitude of the student himself. 'I've had to give up everything for this,' said one very promising member of a French course, director of a plastics firm, in which, it must also be said, his personal stake was high.

There is, then, some resistance to the idea that intensive courses are essential, on the grounds that they are often impracticable.[1] This does not mean that those who have given

---

[1] Many intensive courses are, of course, arranged with much thought and labour for business executives all over the country, particularly where language laboratories are available. The Shell centre prefers courses to last one month, the student attending for an eight-hour day five days a week. At the Institute of Directors there is a similar conviction.

the matter thought underestimate the task of learning a new language. On the contrary, this is partly why a simple answer to the problems of industry seems unattainable.

'There is no magical short route to learning a foreign language, for it demands long and often painful study—and that study must be continuous and should go hand in hand with the opportunity to practise the language being learned in the country of its origin', is the conclusion of *RTB* (cf. previously). *Little-woods* call for 'a commercial "package deal" in language instruction', adaptable for firms such as their own.

10. *Dissatisfaction*. There is evidence of self-questioning and of dissatisfaction with what has so far been done by industry and commerce.

'We have made some progress in language training but more needs to be done' *RTB*.

'We are touching only the fringes of language-learning' (*ibid.*).

In any case, so far as the larger firms are concerned, it is still not unusual to encounter the complaint that the linguistic ability already available within the organization is not being used to full advantage. (Recommendation 2 of the FBI Report is relevant here.) One meets the chemist, who it so happens knows practically no French (this is by no means true of all chemists) but who is being sent off to set up an entire new factory in France after seven weeks' part-time instruction, apparently regarded as sufficient.

With regard to finance, also, there seems to be inconsistency. Industry in general declares the problem of language training to be urgent but when it comes to extra expenditure, individual firms vary considerably in their estimate of the importance of the urgency. Even Shell, whose provision is princely compared with that of most companies, was described as 'cost-conscious'.

It may be, of course, that short of embarking on an immensely expensive combined operation, industrialists recognize that a policy of seeking piece-meal remedies within industry itself can not fail to be inadequate. One company at least appears to have come to this conclusion:

'I appreciate the need for a more wholehearted approach to language instruction but I think *the real answer is that we should rely on more being done in the schools* and recruit into the organisation those who already have a reasonable knowledge of a language on which they can build with further experience', says Mr. N. G. Treloar of BICC, rightly or wrongly tossing the ball back to those who have it in their power to do something about the long-term measures advocated in the still-relevant FBI Report.

The findings of a second FBI working party, *Foreign Language needs of Industry* July 1964, continue however to urge the importance of short-term remedies, stressing also that teachers need training (p. 17), college timetables should be flexible (p. 19) and special courses, not so far available, must be prepared to meet individual needs (p. 19 and *passim*).

Discussion of the last point with teachers of business men at a provincial College of Commerce yielded an interesting suggestion. The Ministry directive of March 1964 states that the cost of special courses shall be borne by the firms concerned. At present, those full-time tutors who actually teach the courses have, on grounds of administrative economy, timetables too overloaded to allow thorough preparation of anything, however special. Part-time staff have no contract, are hired and fired at a moment's notice according to demand and they receive pitiable fees. Yet, by now, some tutors of both kinds have valuable experience of the language needs of firms whose personnel they teach. Subsidized for an adequate period and with the approval of their superiors they would be capable of producing the tailored courses so much needed. Devising good courses takes time. Unless a national research project is undertaken, this approach seems one which industry and commerce might now find it profitable to investigate.

Examinations Available to Adults[1]

P. H. HARGREAVES

THE case for and against the use of examinations in non-vocational fields of study is regularly debated. The most interesting recent study of the problem is the Beloe Report published in 1960 by HMSO. Although this report is concerned with school problems, many of its findings and suggestions are relevant to work with adults.

Outside the university system the following eight examining bodies—including four regional examining boards recognized by the Ministry of Education—offer their services to adults studying modern languages: *The Institute of Linguists* (sixteen languages at five levels); *The Pitman Examinations Institute* (four languages at three levels); *The Royal Society of Arts* (twelve languages at three levels); *The London Chamber of Commerce* (six languages at three levels); *The Northern Counties Technical Examinations Council* (eight languages at six levels); *The Union of Educational Institutes* (three languages at four levels); *The East Midland Educational Union* (four languages at four levels); *The Union of Lancashire and Cheshire Institutes* (five languages at six levels). The number of examinations provided by each board varies from year to year according to student demand; students can never be sure of continuity.

Oral Tests

The Pitman Examinations Institute is alone in not officially prescribing a form of oral test at some if not all levels of its

---

[1] Mr. Hargreaves wishes to thank the National Institute of Adult Education for permission to draw on material contained in his more detailed investigations published in *Adult Education*, Vol. XXXIV, No. 1. May 1961 and No. 5. January 1962.

examinations. However, the significance of the mark awarded for oral work is not always stated plainly and in only three cases, namely the Institute of Linguists (at all levels), the London Chamber of Commerce (at all levels) and the Royal Society of Arts (at two levels), is it made quite clear that a certificate will not be awarded for success in the written test alone. Secondly, there is considerable variation in the use made of external examiners, and it is obvious that there is often little supervision either of the material used or of the manner of awarding marks. No advantage seems to be taken of magnetic tapes, an excellent means of ensuring that oral and written tests receive the same consideration. All this points to a lack of proper regard for the spoken language. In any case, the situation is again subject to annual change.

Written Tests

It is generally agreed that all examining bodies award a disproportionately high percentage of marks to the written part of the examination and that there are no signs of a change for the better. The actual distribution of the marks is normally confidential so as to discourage candidates from concentrating their preparatory learning on only some aspects of the syllabus. All examinations are, however, remarkably similar in pattern. There is no place for translation of verse or for the type of comprehension test requiring answers in English. Grammar tests and comprehension tests lose popularity in the higher levels, which consist almost exclusively of translation and composition. Thus, although it is widely recognized that prose translation into the foreign language can be bad for teacher and student alike, from a certain level onwards it is a compulsory part of every Board's papers. Comprehension tests are obviously not con- sidered suitable for advanced students, although comprehension must be one of the primary aims of all language tuition.

Ideally, it is clear that written examinations should aim at inculcating good linguistic habits. Tests based on accurate comprehension and rapid expression are far more desirable than the traditional hang-over from classical education to be seen annually in the papers prepared for adults. Moreover, although testing devices should not, in theory, affect teaching techniques, teachers do all too often submit to their influence and the students' progress is retarded in consequence.

Conclusion

Examining Boards are not keeping abreast of the times and, far from encouraging desirable developments, are hampering them. The reason usually offered for this state of affairs is financial—they do not have the money to organize adequate oral examinations or to conduct the necessary research into this neglected field. If they increase their fees they will have fewer candidates and this will result in a further lowering of standards. In the meantime, therefore, they carry on in their own way.

Some Examination Papers Examined

O. EISNER

> Hans had laboured for his master seven years, and then he
> spake to him saying: 'Master, my time has run its course, now
> I would fain repair back to my mother, and wilt thou render me
> my meed!' The master, replying, said: 'Thou hast truly
> laboured for me and served me honestly; as was thy labour,
> so shall be thy reward.' So saying, he handed him a lump of
> gold the size of which was like Hans' head. Out of his pocket
> Hans gathered his little cloth wherein he wrapped his gold
> which he placed on his shoulders, and he set out to make his
> way home. As he was thus trotting along, ever setting one leg
> before the other, into his view came a horseman who was
> cheerily riding past on his frisky palfrey. 'Marry,' Hans
> exclaimed quite loudly, 'what a fine thing it is riding on
> horseback!'

THIS is a rendering of a 129-word passage in German—which, incidentally, contained two gross printing errors—set for translation into English by candidates taking an examination after one year's part-time study. The examining board in question, the Institute of Linguists, aims not only at high standards but at modernity, at an unrivalled emphasis on the contemporary, spoken language. Yet the above piece of artificial English is a fair approximation of the style of the German original, a fragment of the well-known story of *Hans im Glück* told by Grimm (or some other adaptor) in that archaizing nineteenth-century German that seeks to convey the flavour of early New High German. The doubtful literary value of such an enterprise is not our concern here; suffice it to say that this kind of language is an artefact and that it is to be hoped it is not being taught to beginners anywhere.

Nor is the passage exceptional. In the same year, the piece to be translated into English by second-year students under the same examining body consisted of seventy-four words (in two sentences) taken from the romanticist German *Taugenichts*, nearly two centuries old.

Both passages are characterized by an unrealistic setting, divorced from everyday life in any age, let alone the twentieth century, and by valueless phraseology such as *Nachtlager; so fort gewandert; wo die Morgensonne so lustig zwischen den Bäumen hindurch schimmerte;* all occurring in the second passage.

The effect of such translation work is a deliberate blunting of the student's sense of style. It is disturbing to those teachers who, refreshed by the wind of change, have abandoned the teaching of out-of-date nineteenth-century versions of the foreign language and are endeavouring to base their work upon frequency of vocabulary and idiom and upon structure.

In the same papers, the passages for translation into German do not make amends for these inadequacies. Thus, for the first-year students, the prose passage (110 words) tells once more of a 'master'.

> 'He spoke as friendly to us as he did to his little children . . . my mother loved him very much . . . he brought a piece of sugar for my mother . . . he always stroked her. . . . All the horses came to him but I think we were his favourites . . . my mother took him to the town.'

For most candidates, only the final sentence would at last solve the mystery—the speaker is Black Beauty. A practical joke? An intelligence test? Certainly no way to examine beginners in German trying to learn the contemporary, spoken language.

Similarly, the prose for the second-year paper (100 words) is a jocular report, again very much in the style of a hundred years ago. Moreover, not only is it shorter than the first-year passage by ten words but its constructions are confined to three easy relative clauses whereas the *Black Beauty* excerpt for the lower grade contains a subordinate clause introduced by 'when', an undoubted stumbling-block for at least half the candidates.

Committed as they mostly are to preparing students for this sort of examination, what must be the reactions of teachers in institutes of further education to such unrealistic, capricious papers (unfortunately by no means confined to one language)? The best of them feel obliged, quite simply, to ignore the examinations. They struggle to impart as good a knowledge of the language in its actual, present-day form as they can, in the hope that this will at the same time enable students to solve examination teasers by virtue of intelligent guesswork. To follow any lead which might be deduced from the papers themselves would surely be irresponsible since it would amount to teaching a dead language deliberately, for the sake of submitting to an unfathomable examination policy.

Index

Administrators, ix, xi, xx; not usually linguists, 116; naming of classes, 116; indifference of, 117, 139

ADULT EDUCATION, ix, 140

Adult education, institutions of, xv (*See also* Non-vocational)

Adult students: characteristics, xvii–xx; age, xiv; education, xiv; socio-economic group, xiv; sex, xvi–xvii; motivation, xvii, 11, 100, 101, 105, 107, 123, 137; ultimate responsibility of, ix, 105, 123, 137; in language laboratory, 33; radio audience, 54–56, 63; wastage, 111; amateur attitude, 112; military personnel, 125; industry, 136–137

ANNAN REPORT on the teaching of Russian, xx, 4, 105, 106

Association of Teachers of Russian, 4

Aural and audio-visual aids, ix, 11, 18–19, 41–42; for advanced students, 82, 83; textbook needs, 116; the Army, 124, 127; self-monitoring, 124, 130, 134; industry, 134 (*See also* Language laboratory)

BBC language courses; history of, 53–54; details, 65–68; use in adult education as a whole, 64 (*See also* Radio)

Beaconsfield: Army School, 123; intensive Russian, 125

BELOE REPORT 1960, 140

British Aluminium Company Limited, 127

British Association for Industrial and Commercial Education, 128

British Insulated Callendar's Cables Limited (BICC), 127, 139

Brooks, Nelson, 34

Cambridge, University of, 130

Catford, J. C., 16, 17

Centre de Recherches et d'Etudes pour la diffusion du Français St Cloud, 26, 36ff.

Chorley, P. R., 132, 134

Civilization: study of, xi, 31, 52, 60, 87; through language, 87, 91; experimental extramural course, syllabus, 92–98; cultural background in technical training, 103 (*See also* Language teaching, liberal approach)

Colleges of Commerce, xv, 100, 117, 128; courses for industry, 134–136

Command of a language, difficulty in defining, 8

Commerce (*See* Industry and commerce)

Commercial Colleges, 100, 117, 128; courses for industry, 134–136

Common Market negotiations, 129

Darbyshire, A. E., 109

Discussion groups, 79–80, 94, 98, 132

APPROACHES TO ADULT TEACHING

edited by NORMAN DEES, B.A.

Director of Extra-Mural Studies, University of Glasgow

The techniques and methods appropriate to the teaching of adults are still a matter of much discussion in educational circles; this book describes the experiences and methods of one university department, and whilst the conclusions contained in it are not flawless, it will certainly provide an interesting basis for further discussion.

The contributors are all full-time or part-time lecturers of the University of Glasgow Department of Extra-Mural Education, and much of the material forms the basis of a current course of lectures and discussions on Adult Education organized and conducted by that department. The processes of adult learning and teaching are described against a background of the history of the adult education movement from the 18th century to the present day. The introductory survey and the discussion of the general nature of adult education are followed by detailed discussions of teaching methods and the attitudes of adult audiences in some of the more important subject categories of adult education provision. The emphasis throughout is on the problems of the teaching and learning of different subjects offered as adult courses, and the book will be of particular value to those actually engaged in adult education; the broad approach to the subject will also make it of interest to the general reader.

TECHNIQUES OF TEACHING

VOLUME 1: PRIMARY EDUCATION
VOLUME 2: SECONDARY EDUCATION
VOLUME 3: TERTIARY EDUCATION

edited by **A. D. C. PETERSON, O.B.E., M.A.**
Director of the Department and Institute of Education,
University of Oxford

The three volumes of 'Techniques of Teaching' cover the primary, secondary and tertiary stages of education respectively, and each is to some extent an independent whole. The work surveys the methods of teaching currently in use, both 'traditional' and 'progressive', at all levels from the infant school to the university. The individual chapters have therefore been written by a wide variety of experts. The emphasis throughout is on the approach to the learning situation from the point of view of the teacher rather than that of the pupils, and of particular interest is the discussion of methods of correspondence education.

The volumes are intended mainly for practising teachers who are interested to know more of what goes on in other subjects or at other levels from their own, and for students of education who require a broad view of educational practice as well as theory. They will also be of interest to administrators, to parents and to those who are interested in what teachers in these different settings are trying to do.